ROBERT HOLMAN

Robert Holman was born in 1952 and brought up on a farm in North Yorkshire. He was awarded an Arts Council Writers' Bursary in 1974, and since then he has spent periods as resident dramatist with the Royal National Theatre and with the Royal Shakespeare Company in Stratford-upon-Avon. He has written extensively for both theatre and television, and his stage plays, including *Outside the Whale*, *German Skerries*, for which he won the George Devine Award, *Other Worlds*, *Today*, *Making Noise Quietly*, *Across Oka* and *Rafts and Dreams*, have been seen in cities as far apart as Los Angeles and Tokyo, following their premieres at such theatres as the Royal Court, the RSC, the Bush and the Edinburgh Traverse. His first novel, *The Amish Landscape*, was published in 1992.

Other titles in this series

Jez Butterworth
MOJO

Caryl Churchill
BLUE HEART
CHURCHILL PLAYS: THREE
CHURCHILL: SHORTS
CLOUD NINE
HOTEL
ICECREAM
LIGHT SHINING IN
BUCKINGHAMSHIRE
MAD FOREST
THE SKRIKER
TRAPS

John Clifford
LIGHT IN THE VILLAGE

Ariel Dorfman
DEATH AND THE MAIDEN
READER
WIDOWS
THE RESISTANCE TRILOGY

David Edgar
DR JEKYLL AND MR HYDE
EDGAR: SHORTS
PENTECOST
THE SHAPE OF THE TABLE

Helen Edmundson
ANNA KARENINA
THE CLEARING
THE MILL ON THE FLOSS
WAR AND PEACE

Kevin Elyot
THE DAY I STOOD STILL
MY NIGHT WITH REG

Peter Flannery
SINGER

Pam Gems
DEBORAH'S DAUGHTER
STANLEY

Tony Kushner
ANGELS IN AMERICA
Parts One and Two

Stephen Jeffreys
THE CLINK
A GOING CONCERN
THE LIBERTINE

Larry Kramer
THE DESTINY OF ME
THE NORMAL HEART

Mike Leigh
ECSTASY
SMELLING A RAT

Clare McIntyre
MY HEART'S A SUITCASE
& LOW LEVEL PANIC

Conor McPherson
THIS LIME TREE BOWER
ST NICHOLAS & THE WEIR
THE WEIR

Terence Rattigan
AFTER THE DANCE
THE BROWNING VERSION
FRENCH WITHOUT TEARS
THE WINSLOW BOY

ROBERT HOLMAN

Bad Weather

NICK HERN BOOKS
LONDON

A Nick Hern Book

Bad Weather first published in Great Britain as an original paperback in 1998 by Nick Hern Books Limited, 14 Larden Road, London W3 7ST, in association with the Royal Shakespeare Company

Cover image: Paul Popplewell and Susan Engel. Photograph by Clare Park, The Special Photographer's Company

Typeset by Country Setting, Woodchurch, Kent TN26 3TB
Printed in England by Cox & Wyman Ltd, Reading, Berks

ISBN 185459 324 2

A CIP catalogue record for this book is available from the British Library

Introduction

Aggravation. Scuffle. A fight at a local Chinese restaurant in Middlesbrough. A man is injured badly. Two young men are involved but only one ends up in prison. Escape for the other, of sorts, yet it is a freedom full of burden. Out of the blue, a figure from the family past arrives and another kind of escape is on offer as *Bad Weather* moves from what appears to be familiar territory into a new and sometimes astonishing landscape.

It is Robert Holman's third play to be produced by the Royal Shakespeare Company and, like *Today* (1984) and *Across Oka* (1988), it is being given its premiere in The Other Place, the company's small auditorium in Stratford-upon-Avon. Much of Holman's work has been seen to startling effect in small theatres because, as in *Bad Weather*, he reveals the larger picture beyond through small and often domestic detail, driven by sharp observation of life rather than a particular ideology and by a deceptive economy of style that is spare and steely, yet compassionate and emotionally powerful.

Born in 1952 in Guisborough, a market town in Yorkshire's Cleveland Hills, and brought up in a Quaker environment, Holman wrote his first play as a school homework while in the sixth form. His English teacher introduced him to a director, Chris Parr, who in 1972 directed a short play of Holman's, *The Grave Lovers*, at The Pool, Edinburgh. Parr became a champion of Holman's work; in 1973 he directed another short play, *Coal*, and, in 1974, as a Sunday night production without décor at the Royal Court, the full-length *Mud*, set in the Cleveland Hills. This led to Holman being awarded an Arts Council playwriting bursary and allowed him to give up his job at a bookstall in Paddington Station – the first job he had come across when he travelled to London having had a spell collecting the dole in Yorkshire after briefly working on a local farm managed by his father.

By the time of the bursary, Holman had written two large-scale plays for the Teeside Youth Theatre, which were performed in the crypt of Middlesbrough Town Hall, a pantomime for The Pool called *Geni Longford Reports*, *The Natural Cause*, which was seen at the Cockpit Theatre, London, and *Moby Dick*, which was produced at the newly-opened Bracknell Arts Centre in Berkshire. He subsequently wrote two plays for Edinburgh's Traverse Theatre which were directed by Chris Parr, who was appointed artistic director in 1975: these were *Outside the Whale* (1976), which dramatised conflicts in the life of George Orwell, and *Rooting* (1979), which, among other things, was notable for the live pigs that featured in its cast. *Outside the Whale* was later seen in London at the Bush Theatre, where in 1977 Parr directed *German Skerries*, set in Yorkshire on the sea cliffs at the mouth of the River Tees. This tender and humorous play brought Holman to wider attention and won him the George Devine award as well as a two-year residency at the National Theatre. He adapted *Emigrés* by the Polish writer Sławomir Mrożek for a NT production at the Young Vic.

As one of the Bush's major writers, he was also the author of *The Estuary*, seen at the theatre in 1980, and of three important short plays in which chance and war, in the shape of the Second World War, the Holocaust and the Falklands, cast their shadow over the characters' lives. They were produced together at the Bush in 1986 as *Making Noise Quietly*, a title which could itself stand as an apt description of Holman's work.

Holman was also commissioned by London's main new play theatre, the Royal Court. In 1983 it presented *Other Worlds*, his first full production there. A rich, humane play drawn on a larger canvas, it is set on the north Yorkshire coast towards the end of the eighteenth century where rivalry between a fishing and a farming community turns violent as they face the prospect of invasion by Napoleon's forces. Holman's association with the Royal Court led to *The Overgrown Path* (1985) and *Rafts and Dreams* (1990), in which the world for the young woman at its centre becomes one huge lake. It is another of his delicately drawn but robust plays that belies the common notion that his considerable skill in observation makes him a purely naturalistic writer.

He has also written television plays – *Mucking Out* (1979), *Chance of a Lifetime* (1980), *Summer's Awakening* (1983) and *This is History, Gran* (1986) – as well as a novel, *The Amish Landscape* (1992), which was inspired by a visit he made to the USA.

His first contact with the Royal Shakespeare Company came when he was commissioned to write a play for a specific group of actors who were in the company at Stratford-upon-Avon. He lived there for a couple of months at the beginning of the season, eating and drinking with the actors and watching them in rehearsal. Within a few months he had written *Today*, which uses the Spanish civil war as a focus for an exploration of class, sexuality, identity and commitment. It was staged before the season ended.

Today spans the years 1920–1946 and takes the audience from Yorkshire to Spain via Cambridge and Twickenham. *Bad Weather* is set in a completely different and contemporary milieu, although, again, there is a shift of location, this time to France. The play nevertheless picks up several earlier themes, from the importance of place and its relationship to personality to the clash of values enmeshed in class, gender, age and culture. Holman examines the sense of otherness within and asks how we see our dreams and ambitions, and what happens to us when they are thwarted by a society that excludes the majority of its people from the economic and cultural means to articulate, let alone realise, them.

The alienation shown in *Bad Weather* is not, however, nihilistic, nor is it in tune with the degradation of fashionable chic. In fact his understanding of human behaviour has never been fashionable; many of his contemporaries were writing political plays of social realism at a time when Holman's anger was not channelled through portrayals of industrial conflict or desolate urban wastelands but through highly nuanced and sensitive portraits of individuals under stress. He has continued in that vein, and in *Bad Weather* vital issues are present, as they always have been, not formed as a rhetorical statement on the state of the nation but as an urgent and insistent statement on the state of its individual and neglected citizens.

Colin Chambers

Bad Weather was first performed by the Royal Shakespeare Company at The Other Place, Stratford-upon-Avon, on 22 April 1998. The cast, in order of appearance, was as follows:

RHONA	Emma Handy
LUKE	Paul Popplewell
JAMIE	Ryan Pope
KAY	Susan Brown
NOEL	Barry Stanton
AGNES	Susan Engel

Director Steven Pimlott
Designer Ashley Martin-Davis
Lighting Designer Hugh Vanstone
Sound Andrea J. Cox
Assistant Director Alison Sutcliffe
Company Voice Work Andrew Wade and Lyn Darnley
Production Manager Mark Graham
Costume Supervisor Carrie Baylis

Stage Manager Maggie Mackay
Deputy Stage Manager Suzi Blakey
Assistant Stage Manager Stephen Cressy

The text published here is as it was on the first day of rehearsal.

BAD WEATHER

Characters

RHONA

LUKE

JAMIE

KAY TONNERRE

NOEL

AGNÈS COLLIN

Act One

Scene 1 Middlesbrough

Scene 2 Outside the Crown Court

Scene 3 The flats

Scene 4 The flats

Scene 5 The shops

Scene 6 The shops

Act Two

Scene 1 Deerbolt

Scene 2 France

Scene 3 The château

Scene 4 The Tees estuary

Scene 5 The château

Scene 6 Deerbolt

The play takes place in the present day

ACT ONE

Scene One

A near-derelict parade of shops on a modern housing estate in Middlesbrough. An evening in March.

There is a betting shop which is permanently boarded up with metal shutters so that it looks closed forever, when during the day it is open. A grocers next to it is similarly covered in graffiti. It has wooden shutters and a steel door. Next to the grocers is a Chinese chip shop, the Red Lanterns, which is open. Fluorescent light is spilling out through the window. On the concrete forecourt in front of the shops is a metal rubbish bin. It is black from having been set on fire.

RHONA *is waiting. She is seventeen years old with a pinched white face. Her blonde hair is tied back. She is wearing her best gaberdine and she has a shoulder bag.*

LUKE *enters. He is twenty-one years old, small and wiry with his hair cut so short that his head is almost shaved. He has a gold ear stud. He is wearing jeans and a white sweatshirt.*

LUKE. Yer waitin' for the end, our kid?

RHONA. End of what? Yer don't make sense when yer try hard, you.

LUKE *puts his hands behind his back.*

LUKE. Which hand d'yer want?

RHONA. I don't want none of them.

LUKE *holds out a hand. He lets a silver chain and crucifix dangle down from his palm.*

That don't impress us at all.

LUKE. It's silver.

RHONA. So what?

LUKE. Like all good stuff it's worth more than it looks.

RHONA. Yer think I care?

LUKE. Solid silver.

RHONA. Sell it then.

LUKE. It's hallmarked. I will if you don't want it.

RHONA. I don't.

LUKE. It'd look pretty on yer, our lass. It's antique an' all.

He puts the crucifix in his pocket.

Never tell us I'm not generous. Next time yer think I'm mean yer'll have something to remember.

RHONA *walks a few feet, looking off towards the flats.*

Yer waitin' for Jamie?

RHONA. What's it to you?

LUKE. It's nowt to me.

RHONA. Exactly. Go and do yer crowing somewhere else.

LUKE. Is that what I'm doing?

RHONA. I've heard you sounding off, not that I need to.

LUKE. Jamie's my friend as well.

RHONA. Some friend you are.

LUKE. Yeh, I am.

RHONA. What's happened today, if you care so much?

LUKE. I don't keep abreast of it, our kid.

RHONA. You haven't a clue.

LUKE. It's best all round.

RHONA. Yer don't even think about 'im being in court, d'yer? I've not seen yer there givin' support. Yer noticeable by your absence, you.

LUKE. He's out on bail, what yer on about. I think more than you, about more than you.

He kicks a discarded lager can into the shutters of the betting shop.

RHONA. I've stood in the witness box today because of you, Luke.

LUKE. Yer reckon yer unique? We've all done that, Rhona. D'yer want a medal to wear or something?

He looks at his sister.

He'll be all right. It's more than a certainty. Yer get bothered too much. Yer want to relax more.

RHONA. I really hate you.

LUKE. No, yer don't.

JAMIE *enters hurrying, slightly out of breath. He is nineteen years old with a fresh complexion and short hair. He is wearing jeans and a cagoule.*

LUKE *dribbles the lager can.*

D'yer fancy comin' down to the Belladonna for the night, Jamie?

JAMIE. It's up to Rhona. She makes the decisions.

RHONA. I've told 'im already to get lost. You go with 'im and that's it.

JAMIE. We'd better not like.

RHONA. Yer'd drink the river empty if there was alcohol in it, you would.

LUKE. Tell us who'd be inconvenienced?

JAMIE *and* RHONA *meet.*

JAMIE. She gave us ten. It's all she had.

LUKE. Yer gettin' money from yer mam?

JAMIE. Yeh.

He gives two five pound notes to RHONA.

LUKE. Is it English?

RHONA. What yer on about?

LUKE. Could be notes in francs.

RHONA. You don't know half the time.

LUKE. Yer should laugh more, our lass.

LUKE *picks up the can. He throws it into the air and heads it into the rubbish bin.*

RHONA *takes a purse from her bag and puts the money inside it.*

LUKE *puts his arm around* JAMIE*'s neck.*

How's it all going then, kidda?

JAMIE. Not bad, I hope. It's a bit scary sometimes.

RHONA. Get yer hand off him.

JAMIE. It depends on the day, doesn' it?

RHONA *nods.*

She was dead terrific this morning. It was brilliant. Yer'd never 'ave guessed she was lying.

LUKE. I walk around with me toes crossed for yer.

RHONA. Give it a rest, Luke. It's not you in the dock.

LUKE. Me sister gets serious, 'ave yer noticed?

RHONA. He's doin' this for you.

LUKE. How's the old judge doing?

JAMIE *shrugs.*

JAMIE. All right, I think.

RHONA. It's not all right. He's biased.

JAMIE. He's in the middle of summing up, yer know.

LUKE. There's no evidence.

JAMIE. There is.

RHONA. You've not heard it. The judge has made it all wrong.

LUKE. Keep t'yer story, won't yer?

JAMIE. I have done.

LUKE. Forever.

RHONA. I had to lie thanks t'you.

LUKE. I sleep well.

RHONA. The only time you'll sleep well is when yer dead, and not even then.

JAMIE. I'm not a grass.

RHONA. Yer know he's innocent.

LUKE. We're all innocent.

RHONA. You're not. You kicked 'im in the face. He was nowhere near.

LUKE. Yer might as well 'ave done all the kicking, eh Jamie?

JAMIE. I don't know.

RHONA. I do. 'E wouldn't do owt like that. Never.

LUKE. Yer like the judge, our lass, yer biased.

RHONA. It don't matter. You kicked his head in. Jamie didn't.

She walks away.

I can't stand you.

JAMIE *looks at* LUKE.

JAMIE. I might go down tomorrow, yer know. It's possible.

LUKE. Yer nervous?

JAMIE *nods.*

JAMIE. Yeh, really nervous.

RHONA. You don't see 'im every day. We're all scared.

LUKE. It's up to the jury.

JAMIE. Yeh.

KAY TONNERRE *enters from the flats. She is forty-four years old with a round face and a dark complexion. There is a dignity about her that is unforced. She is wearing a coat which is unfastened.*

JAMIE. Yer don't 'ave to check on us, Mum.

RHONA. Have you two had a row?

KAY. I'm worried about you, Rhona.

RHONA. We're not going to the Belladonna or owt like that.

KAY. I hope you're not.

RHONA. Yer didn't tell us yer'd had an argument.

JAMIE *shrugs.*

JAMIE. We didn't.

KAY. Make him see sense, Luke.

LUKE. It's nowt to do with me like.

KAY. This is about the most important night of his life. You owe it to him, and you owe it to me to be sensible. All of you.

LUKE. I don't owe anybody anything. I never will.

He takes the crucifix from his pocket.

I only came to give yer this.

RHONA. Don't take it. He tried to give it to us.

LUKE. Give it to one of yer, that's all.

RHONA. Yer didn't even know what was happening.

LUKE. Yer expect us to be clairvoyant?

JAMIE *takes the crucifix. He fastens the chain around* RHONA*'s neck.*

RHONA. I don't want it.

JAMIE. Yer've got it. I do. I want t'think of yer wearing it tomorrow.

RHONA *looks at the crucifix.*

RHONA. I suppose it is pretty.

LUKE. Yer comin' down the Belladonna then?

RHONA. Yer know this could be 'is last night, don't yer?

LUKE. It's not. Yer talking rubbish and yer all reckonin' on worse.

RHONA *goes towards* KAY.

RHONA. Yer always said they were stupid. They get more stupid every minute in my opinion.

KAY. Yes. I don't suppose he'll listen to you, but he might.

KAY *gives* RHONA *a ten pound note. She looks at* JAMIE.

I'd put it away in a tin, I'd forgotten.

RHONA *shows him the money.*

RHONA. Another ten.

KAY *exits.*

JAMIE. We could go for a bit.

RHONA. Yer go without us then. I'm not going.

LUKE. What's wrong with yer?

RHONA. Nothing, and I wouldn't tell you if there was.

LUKE. Dance the night to oblivion. Yer deserve it.

RHONA *puts the money in her purse.* JAMIE *looks at* LUKE.

JAMIE. I didn't want to be late back anyway.

LUKE. The jury's not goin' t'find yer guilty.

RHONA. You know so little about so much, you.

LUKE. I won't be standing up in court, ever.

RHONA. Yer should be.

LUKE. Everywhere yer look there's a should be, our lass. It makes no difference.

RHONA. Yer threaten all people but me, you do.

LUKE. I threaten no one. No one.

JAMIE. I hate it when you two fight.

RHONA. Yer hate us a lot then, that's all I can say. He nearly died that bloke after you kicked him.

LUKE. I bet he's walking around like it never went on.

LUKE *strikes a match. He uses it to light a whole box of matches. He puts the box into the rubbish bin. Smoke starts to come out of it.*

JAMIE. We could go for an hour.

RHONA. It's a waste of money for an hour.

LUKE. Yer can be miserable on yer own. If yer going to be miserable yer might as well be with us. Yer care too much.

RHONA. Someone has to. Aren't you cold?

LUKE. Yer something else, our kid.

RHONA. Yer never wear that jacket I got yer. There was a mix up with the prices. That's why it was cheaper. It was a mistake.

LUKE. I'll put it on tonight, just for you.

RHONA. Yer won't.

LUKE. Yer'll believe me when you see me.

RHONA. I will an' all.

JAMIE *goes to her. He takes her hand.*

How'll we get back?

JAMIE. On the bus. Or walk like usual.

RHONA. Why don't we go tomorrow?

JAMIE. I'm trying not to think about tomorrow.

RHONA. I know. I'm doing it for both of us.

JAMIE *nibbles her ear.*

We're being daft and really stupid.

LUKE. Give over listenin' to his mam. There's only so many words yer can hear in a lifetime. Yer using yours up dead rapidly. Yer'll find there's none left over. Then where will yer be? Yer'll be on yer own. Yer don't regret what yer do. Not me. I don't. Yer regret what yer should 'ave done, but didn't do.

RHONA. Are you coming to court in the morning?

LUKE. All right.

RHONA. That means yer'll change yer mind.

LUKE. I'll get me stuff. I'll meet yer back here.

LUKE *exits.*

JAMIE *and* RHONA *look at one another. They start to kiss.*

Scene Two

The street outside the court. Late afternoon the following day.

A stone building. Above the entrance-way is a piece of sandstone with the title The Crown Court cut into it. The pavement is wet. There is a lamp-post.

KAY *comes out of the wooden doors and down the steps. She stops by the lamp. The afternoon is overcast, dark enough for her to be lit slightly by the sodium light. She is wearing her best clothes, a dress and a coat which is unfastened.*

NOEL *comes out of the building and walks away. He is fifty-eight years old, rotund with a beer belly, and slightly scruffily dressed in trousers, a shirt with the top button undone, and a plain dark jacket.*

As he has walked away, KAY *has taken him in. He has seen her. He slows down. He stops, pauses, and then turns.*

KAY *hesitates.*

KAY. Were you for him or against him?

NOEL *hesitates.*

NOEL. I'm not supposed to say. There were notices up all over the jury room.

KAY. It's all right, he knows. He knows you were for him.

A slight pause.

NOEL. Are you his mother?

KAY. Yes.

NOEL. A lot of it didn't make sense to me. Yer should get 'im to appeal.

He goes towards her, tentatively.

Was he there that night at the Red Lanterns? I suppose I shouldn't ask. Yer don't have to say.

KAY. As far as I know he was there, but he didn't do anything wrong.

NOEL. There was at least one other person.

KAY. Yes. Luke Dangerfield.

NOEL. Why wasn't he charged?

KAY. No one would give statements to the police, no one would give evidence. The judge doesn't understand that boys of their age hang about on street corners.

NOEL. I know.

RHONA *comes out of the building, followed by* LUKE. LUKE *is wearing trousers and a shirt. He hangs back on the steps.* RHONA *has her shoulder bag and is wearing the crucifix. She joins* KAY *who is with* NOEL.

KAY. This is the juror who was for him.

RHONA. Hello.

NOEL. Hello.

RHONA *hesitates.*

You do what yer've got to do, love. Don't mind me.

RHONA. They're going to ask if we can see 'im. They don't think they'll let us. Someone 'as said they reckon he'll probably go to Deerbolt, near Barnard Castle.

KAY. Who?

RHONA. The solicitor said to the barrister. It's a young offenders' prison, because he's under twenty-one. They're trying to find out.

KAY. Will someone come and let us know?

RHONA *shrugs.*

RHONA. They don't tell yer anything. They know where we are. They know we're out here.

LUKE *lights a cigarette.*

KAY. Rhona's pregnant as well. The two of them have been naughty and done what they shouldn't have done.

NOEL. I don't think we're meant to be talking to each other.

KAY. It doesn't matter now. What difference will it make?

KAY *glances at* LUKE. NOEL *has seen* LUKE *smoking. He takes out a packet of cigarettes and offers them.* KAY *shakes her head.* RHONA *takes one.* NOEL *lights her cigarette before lighting his own.*

NOEL. Let's go over there.

They move away from the door.

I shouldn't say very much, I might be in trouble.

RHONA. He didn't do it, yer know. All Jamie did was spit on 'im. Gob once.

NOEL. Were you there, pet?

RHONA. Yeh. I know I lied in the witness box, said we weren't there when we were. It weren't even grievous bodily harm. He weren't that badly hurt.

NOEL. He was in hospital, for goodness sake.

RHONA. Only for a day. Spit don't hurt.

KAY *runs her hand through her hair.*

KAY. Would you mind if we stopped for a minute? I've no energy for anything.

KAY *faints. She ends up flat on the pavement.*

RHONA. See what you're responsible for. Everything yer do isn't a help.

LUKE. You asked us to come.

RHONA. I didn't mean yer to.

NOEL *squats down.* KAY *is already picking herself up.*

KAY. I'm so sorry. I feel so drained all of a sudden.

NOEL. Yer bound to. Isn't she?

RHONA. Yeh. I feel funny an' all. It's dead weird all this.

KAY *gets up on her own without help.*

RHONA *holds out her hand. It has started spitting with rain. She takes an umbrella from her shoulder bag and puts it up over herself and* KAY.

NOEL. I should be going.

LUKE *opens the door.*

LUKE. The solicitor's calling for yer.

RHONA *gives the umbrella to* KAY. *She hurries to the steps and goes inside.* LUKE *follows her in.*

NOEL. Will yer tell Jamie that one member of the jury cared about him.

KAY. Why?

NOEL. I thought he was innocent.

A slight pause.

Yer white as paper.

He takes the umbrella. He holds it over them.

Yer'd think they'd put some seats somewhere.

LUKE *comes out of the building.*

Does 'e want to share this?

KAY. No.

She adjusts her clothes, brushes off some dirt.

NOEL. Yer've marked yer skirt a bit.

KAY. Where?

NOEL. There.

RHONA *comes out. She goes to* KAY *and* NOEL.

RHONA. He is going to Deerbolt. Tonight.

KAY. What about seeing him?

RHONA. No. The solicitor's still waitin'. There's a real crush. There's not enough guards for all the prisoners. He hasn't been in yet. 'E says it don't matter. 'E says we can talk, there's nowt wrong in it now it's finished.

NOEL *gives the umbrella to* RHONA.

KAY. From the very beginning we imagined it would work out, didn't we? I told the police Jamie had nothing to do with it.

NOEL. It was Mr Wong. I thought of him as Mr Wong. I didn't get 'is name properly. The Chinese guy who owns the Red Lanterns chip shop. It was his evidence.

RHONA. He's nothin' but a liar. He never tells the truth. 'E don't even speak English right.

KAY. His shop has been set on fire. He was threatened again.

She glances at LUKE.

LUKE. Are we going in a minute then like?

KAY. He's frightened.

RHONA. 'E speaks much better English than he was lettin' on in court.

KAY. I do understand. I've tried to. He wouldn't make a statement for a fortnight. Then he said exactly what the police wanted him to say.

A slight pause.

NOEL. Is that where yer go and mess around on Saturday nights?

RHONA. On any night. There's always lots of fights. It's notorious.

KAY. It should stop you going, but it doesn't.

NOEL. We're all supposed to learn by experience, pet.

RHONA. Yeh. The solicitor says we can go. We've to ring him sometime on Monday.

KAY. Is that all?

RHONA. Yeh, that's it.

RHONA *puts out her cigarette. It has stopped raining. She furls the umbrella.*

Where d'yer live?

NOEL. The other side of Middlesbrough.

RHONA. We're from North Ormesby.

NOEL. I know.

RHONA. He started it.

NOEL. Who?

RHONA. The bloke who was kicked. That didn't come out neither. It should have done.

NOEL. How could it?

RHONA. What?

NOEL. It couldn't come out because you claimed you were somewhere else, in the pub.

RHONA. Yeh. The judge didn't listen. You know more about it than he does.

LUKE. See yer around, maybe.

RHONA. Yer won't if I see you first.

LUKE *exits.*

KAY *looks at her watch.*

KAY. There isn't a bus for twenty minutes.

RHONA *puts the umbrella in her bag.*

RHONA. What're yer hanging about us for?

NOEL. I'm concerned, I suppose.

RHONA. Why? It's nowt to do with you anyway.

NOEL. No, that's true.

KAY *walks away. She sits on the steps.* RHONA *looks at the sky.*

RHONA. I wish it'd make up its mind.

NOEL. It's water blowing off the roof.

He glances at KAY.

Will someone be with her tonight?

RHONA. How come yer ask me? How should I know.

NOEL *goes to* KAY. *He sits down beside her.*

KAY. I feel so powerless.

RHONA. Are we going for the bus or what?

NOEL. Don't you ever shut up.

RHONA *gulps.*

RHONA. I didn't say anything much at all.

RHONA *strolls over to them.*

What're yer tellin' us off for?

KAY. It's not your fault, Rhona.

RHONA. That's what the judge said. 'E said I weren't to blame. Yer not part of us, yer not our family. I am nearly.

She sits down, slightly apart from them.

I pulled Jamie off. It was me that got hold of him and stopped him.

KAY *leans forward so that she can see* RHONA.

KAY. Is that what happened?

RHONA. Yeh. I grabbed him.

NOEL. Why didn't you say so in court?

RHONA. I couldn't in a hundred years. They only got Jamie because they were after our lad. They know he didn't do it. They hoped he'd grass on him. It's our brother they wanted to get locked up. It's not honest. It's not proper.

KAY *sits back.*

KAY. I didn't expect this.

RHONA. I bloody did.

RHONA *takes an illustrated book on childbirth from her bag, puts it on her lap and turns the pages.*

They're realistic these photos. I presume they are because they're photos. There's a three month foetus.

A pause.

On the next one yer can see the tiny fingers developing. It's like a baby in a bottle.

RHONA *turns the page.*

KAY. You're the first person who's cared.

RHONA. Yeh, yer are.

KAY. I'll tell Jamie what you said.

RHONA. Yer could complain for us.

NOEL. I'm in the same position as you.

RHONA *turns the page.*

RHONA. It's amazing where they've got the camera. Yer'd think it was on the outside.

She looks at NOEL.

What yer doin' here?

NOEL. I'm trying to be sympathetic, Rhona.

RHONA. Why? What for?

NOEL. I'm not sure.

RHONA. If you're not sure, how will we be.

KAY. Do you have a bus to catch as well?

NOEL. Yes.

A slight pause.

It's on the tip of my tongue to keep asking you if you're feeling any better.

KAY. It's not your problem.

A slight pause.

NOEL. I'd like it to be my problem. I feel. I don't know what I feel. Something for you, yer know. I can't explain it all that well. I'm not very articulate on a good day. I knew you were his mother when I saw you in the public gallery. Something told me. Yer look, yer face.

RHONA. We were watchin' each other.

NOEL. Yes. Something kept telling me something. About you all.

He looks at KAY.

Particularly you.

KAY. Don't be sorry.

RHONA. 'E's not half as sorry as us.

NOEL. Be quiet.

RHONA. I didn't do nowt. Tell us what I did, if yer can. I bet yer can't.

A slight pause.

KAY. I don't know quite what you're saying.

NOEL. I don't either. Don't you?

KAY. No.

RHONA. Why don't yer play twenty questions, and put us all out of our suffering.

KAY. I hate games of that sort, Rhona.

NOEL *is looking at* KAY.

NOEL. So do I.

Scene Three

The high balcony of a tower block flat. A few hours later.

The sun is setting. A ray of sunlight is slanting down, lighting the grey concrete and the metal rail. On the balcony there are some shrivelled pot plants, a folded deckchair, and an old table with some more plants on it. The place is neat and well cared for, though it could do with painting.

KAY *comes out through the sliding glass doors which are already open. She is wearing a man's dressing-gown, has bare feet, and is carrying a glass of lager and a can. She puts them on top of the rail to one side, moves back along and looks out.*

NOEL *comes onto the balcony. He is wearing only his trousers, and his belt needs fastening.*

NOEL. Blimey, you take risks.

He takes hold of the glass and the can.

The flush on your cistern isn't working as it should. It'll be corroded inside. I can fix it if yer want?

KAY. Don't bother about it now.

NOEL. I'd like to bother. It might need a new bit from the plumbers, and I'd have to fetch some tools from home. Unless you've got any?

He drinks.

KAY. The fridge only works about half what it should do as well.

NOEL. It doesn't matter. It's good. It's cold enough.

He looks at her.

Are you not havin' one yerself? I won't stay long, I promise.

KAY. Don't take that as a sign of anything.

NOEL. You are sure?

KAY. Yes.

NOEL *looks out.*

NOEL. I've always had a regard for these flats. A kind of quiet regard since this is the first time I've been in one. No, that's rubbish. I'm talking rubbish. I do appreciate the view yer get though, over the Tees.

KAY *smiles.*

When I was a young lad this area was more notorious than anything. Perhaps yer remember? There were acres of terraced houses that went all the way to the river, to the docks. They pulled them down because it was bad. And they were replaced with something that was meant to be good. I reckon hardship is like water. It finds a level. Violence is pretty much the same.

He looks at her.

I'm sorry. I have this big habit of being ignorant. I'm getting it out of the way so you expect less of me.

KAY. I don't expect anything.

NOEL. Yes, I see that, but I want yer to a bit. I know we didn't make it just now. We could've done another time. It doesn't matter. Not to me.

KAY *smiles.*

You owe me at least something, don't you? I don't know why I reckon yer do, but yer do. I haven't a clue what you're thinking, or what it means. Yer've more capacity for quiet than – I can't think of a thing – a church, I suppose.

KAY. Are you married, Noel?

NOEL. Yes. No, it doesn't stop me. It never has. She's fifteen years older than me.

KAY. What does that make her?

NOEL. Plain.

KAY. I meant her age.

NOEL. I know you did.

He pours more lager into the glass.

Do I drink this quickly? Slowly? You tell us.

KAY. Slowly.

KAY *leans on the rail.*

I don't live with the angels. There's no reason for you to be so polite.

NOEL. Am I being?

KAY. Yes.

A rainbow appears, striking powerful colours across the concrete and the balcony.

NOEL *leans on the rail and looks out.*

NOEL. I'm going back a couple of decades, if not more. Yer forget. When they painted the warehouses at British Steel, a lot of people round here painted their houses. Yer'd go in and out, and they'd all be the same colour. Then there were those who 'ad the audacity to do the outsides, the doors and the windows. It was petty, sort of thing. A pilferer's paradise.

KAY. Where were you born, Noel?

NOEL. A few miles over there, where the river curves round. My Dad – God bless him – was a spot-welder on the docks, so we always had a grubby inside of our house. It was better than this.

He looks at her.

Am I being bloody clumsy?

KAY. Why?

NOEL. Yer don't give yerself away easily. I mean, you're definitely not from here originally. There's more books in there than in a library. I'm kind of makin' a joke of it, but not really. If yer think I'm an idiot, just tell me so we know.

KAY. I don't. I would never think that.

NOEL. I think it about meself sometimes.

KAY *looks out.*

KAY. Have you been in prison?

NOEL. That didn't influence us this afternoon. This didn't either.

KAY *rests her arms on the rail and looks at him.*

Yer canny.

KAY. Am I?

NOEL. Yes, you are. I was in for a few years a long time ago. I was not a saint, unfortunately. Like a lot of people I have to wish that I was. I was young. Younger. Not exactly a boy, but too young to find myself frightening, if yer get what I mean by that? Or understand it. Yer not the only one who can be canny. As you get older it becomes harder to live with yourself. Yer know, with the bits of insight. Yer find yer own personality more alarming. I won't be taken for an idiot.

KAY. Is that what I'm doing?

NOEL. No. Maybe a touch here and there. I don't know. Yes.

A slight pause.

KAY. I'm not doing it on purpose.

A slight pause.

NOEL. All that was selfish of me. Please forget it.

KAY. I don't want to.

NOEL. All I'm doing is proving yer right.

KAY. No.

A slight pause.

NOEL. I wanted to be kind.

KAY. You are.

Silence.

NOEL *puts the glass and the can on the table.*

NOEL. I'd better go.

KAY. Don't. Wait.

NOEL *goes inside. He returns almost immediately having put on his shirt.*

I'm sorry we couldn't fuck.

She runs her fingers through her hair. A tear is about to come out. NOEL *takes hold of her.* KAY *rests her head on the side of his neck. He runs one of his hands up and down her back.*

NOEL. It's my fault.

KAY *straightens up.* NOEL *wipes away a single tear that has run down her cheek. Their hands fumble together, their fingers interlace.*

KAY. I don't know what I'm doing.

NOEL. Yer caught us by surprise.

KAY. I'm making myself be like this.

NOEL. Yer not. It just feels that way. Yer know, when people get upset to be manipulative. It happens.

KAY. Yes.

NOEL. Yer can't expect to be anything else.

KAY. No.

KAY *runs her fingers down his face.*

I'm like an empty shell.

She kisses him. They kiss. KAY *starts to cry.*

I'm so mixed up.

NOEL. Sssh. Sssh.

KAY. Jamie has a string of offences.

NOEL. I know.

KAY. They're not bad offences.

NOEL. They're burglary and shoplifting, and aggravated bodily harm. His antecedence was read out at the end, love. He was bound to get prison this time.

KAY *straightens up.*

I wanted to know something about you that was more than this flat.

She wipes away a few tears with the dressing-gown.

Is that Jamie's?

KAY. Yes. I'm very sorry.

NOEL. What for? Don't be.

KAY *smiles.*

KAY. Do you get lonely sometimes?

NOEL. If I do I go out.

KAY. My best friend lives in France. I was brought up there.

NOEL. Is that why a lot of the books are French? I knew it wasn't a habit yer'd picked up in Middlesbrough.

KAY. I read in French sometimes.

KAY *turns and leans on the rail.*

I had Jamie in Middlesbrough General. You can see it if you know where to look.

NOEL *picks up the glass. He leans on the rail beside her.*

My best friend brought me up. I miss her quite a bit just now.

She puts her hands in the pockets on the dressing-gown.

Are you cold?

NOEL. No. Are you?

KAY. I will be. We'll go in in a minute.

KAY *takes out some condoms.*

I only wish he'd used them.

NOEL. What happened to your mum and dad?

KAY. Oh, nothing much. Or rather a lot.

NOEL. Were they French?

KAY. My father was. My mother was English. I got on very well with my father, until he died. I'm sure that would have continued. He died when I was eleven.

NOEL. It's too young.

KAY. Yes.

NOEL. Is that when all the problems started?

KAY. You're astute. You don't have to go on showing it.

NOEL. I'm intrigued.

KAY *rubs her nose on his nose.*

KAY. Or nosey.

NOEL. I know you don't belong here.

KAY. Don't I?

NOEL. No.

KAY. I am here.

NOEL. Well. Yes.

KAY *takes the glass off him. She drinks. She gives it back to him. A tear comes out and runs down her cheek.*

I was going to ask you if you were better.

KAY. Oh, I'm so useless. I don't know what to do.

She wipes away the tear with her hand.

NOEL. Is there anything I can do?

KAY *shakes her head.*

KAY. No. Stay for a while.

KAY *makes herself smile.*

My father managed and ran a vineyard, which he inherited from my grandfather. Don't laugh at me, will you?

NOEL. If I was laughing you'd hear me.

KAY. All the land and the château that went with it was his. When he died it became mine. He didn't tell me, or my mother. Suddenly I owned a vineyard that had been there for centuries, and was all about tradition, and I was a little girl. It was more or less hopeless. My mother was resentful. I don't know why he'd married her, except that she was very beautiful. More than beautiful actually. She took your breath away. I don't blame him for falling in love with her, but he deserved better. He was good, and she was mad.

NOEL. Why?

KAY. She just was. She was jealous more than anything else. Riddled with it. Jealous of me, jealous of the accountants who brought in an overseer, who she attacked. They gave her money and sent her away. She came back. She'd be sweetness and light, then horrible again. I was left the vineyard, but it wasn't actually mine until I was twenty-four. That's what she used against me. She even tried when I was eleven, but I didn't understand it. She'd say he didn't trust me, and she went on saying it. I didn't have the wherewithal to ask her if it was sensible to leave an eleven year old in charge. Would you?

NOEL. No, I don't suppose so.

KAY. None of it is all that relevant to anything very much. It's not that it's private. It happened and it's finished. I don't rake over it.

NOEL. Where's your mother?

KAY. I don't know and I don't care. Eventually she ran away.

NOEL *smiles.*

NOEL. I painted white lines on roads, and took them off again. Not always on the same day. I was given redundancy.

He puts his arm round her waist.

Was it sad?

KAY. What exactly?

NOEL. Yer father and yer mam and you.

KAY. Yes, I think it was. I look at it now through a kind of mist, which is why I very rarely mention it. I don't know how much Jamie has told Rhona, for instance. It was something that happened. Not to him. Why should he talk about it? Can I ask you not to?

NOEL. Who would I tell? I don't know what to tell.

KAY. In the pub or wherever it is you go.

The rainbow disappears.

NOEL. What did yer mam do?

KAY. There were boyfriends. She lived it up in Paris. She told lies about her wealth. She got married again. And the estate paid her debts. I paid her debts eventually.

NOEL. Why?

KAY. She was my mother. Later on there were hotel bills from Australia and South Africa. She went through a fortune playing roulette. She realised she could. She was right in a way. My father had married her. She had no money and he was rich. She was the beauty from England who he wanted to show off. She won.

NOEL. Yer funny.

KAY. Am I?

NOEL. Not funny. Something other than funny. Who looked after you?

KAY. I had a nanny.

NOEL. The friend?

KAY. Yes. Don't pry, Noel, will you?

NOEL. I don't know. I promise you I won't.

He slowly moves his head and kisses KAY *on the lips.*

Something drops onto the balcony.

KAY. What on earth was that?

NOEL *picks up a small piece of ice.*

NOEL. A hailstone. I remember once. In August. Where was I? I was in the Lake District of all places. They were massive.

A few more hailstones drop out of the sky.

They fell for about thirty seconds. And people had their arms cut if they were wearing short sleeves.

Scene Four

The balcony. Later, in the middle of the night.

The lights of the town, British Steel and the flares of ICI are illuminating the underside of the clouds.

RHONA *is on the balcony.*

NOEL *appears through the open, glass doors. He is wearing* JAMIE*'s dressing-gown.*

NOEL. What're you doing?

RHONA. I could ask you the same thing like.

NOEL. I asked first.

RHONA. I have a key. I let meself in sometimes. It's got nothin' to do with you.

NOEL. You and me, we're always close to getting off on the wrong foot.

RHONA. I'm not bothered. You can take a running jump over a cliff as far as I care. Sooner the better.

RHONA *takes a packet of cigarettes from her coat pocket.*

It's me only one.

NOEL *has a disposable lighter. He lights her cigarette.*

NOEL. I couldn't sleep either.

He has a packet of cigarettes in the dressing-gown. He lights one for himself.

RHONA. Yer must think I'm soft in the head. All yer doin' is taking advantage of her.

NOEL. Am I?

RHONA. Yer not even the second.

NOEL. Second what?

RHONA. Or the third. Everyone takes advantage of 'er. They're queuing up at the door some days. Yer can't get in.

NOEL. Do you?

RHONA. Suppose so.

NOEL *goes along the balcony.* RHONA *perches on top of the rail, on the right angle at the other end.*

NOEL. I didn't know she was born in France.

RHONA. Yer do or yer wouldn't say.

NOEL *smiles.*

What's it to you?

NOEL. I care about her.

RHONA. I bet yer use that word a lot to all your girlfriends.

NOEL. Yer don't have to like me, Rhona.

RHONA. I don't.

A slight pause.

NOEL. Tell me about the vineyard.

RHONA. I only know what Jamie knows. She gave it all to her mam as soon as she could. It only became hers when she was twenty-four. It's what rich people do in their wills. She's no money. That do yer?

KAY *appears in the shadows, behind the doors, where they cannot see her. She is wearing a plain white nightdress which is picking up the light from outside.*

Jamie and me could've been rich, but for her. It's what Jamie says. I say I wouldn't have known him to begin with if he'd been rich. I'd be the same, whichever way yer look at it.
So would you. You will be forever. We all have to win the lottery. I said to Jamie once he should find out more from his

mam. Pump her a bit. Find out about his grandma. Maybe it wasn't all over and settled, yer know. Maybe she kept a bit of it for herself and didn't tell no one. I would. I wouldn't have a secret to keep because I wouldn't have given it away in the first place. It'd all be mine, and Jamie's. We'd have plenty of money. It's a mystery to me how yer get hold of some. She had a fortune. It's the only mystery I'm interested in. They can keep Loch Ness as far as I'm concerned.

KAY. There is no mystery, Rhona.

KAY *disappears for a split second. Immediately the room light comes on. Light spills out onto the balcony.* KAY *comes back.*

RHONA *drops her head.*

RHONA. I'm sorry like.

NOEL. Shall I get you a blanket?

KAY *stops him.*

KAY. I'm going back to bed in a minute.

She looks at RHONA.

I gave the vineyard to Jamie's grandmother. I paid her debts. There is nothing curious about it whatsoever. It wasn't some strange event. Jamie's grandmother sold it. Everything went up for auction. That was her choice. By then it was hers to sell. Jamie is silly.

RHONA. Yeh.

KAY. If you want to, use his room.

RHONA. Can I?

KAY. Yes, of course.

RHONA. Me mam's in a mood again.

KAY. Goodnight.

KAY *goes in.*

A slight pause.

RHONA. Where does yer wife think yer are, if one was daft enough to marry yer?

NOEL. You're not bothered about being liked, are you?

RHONA. I am as matter-of-fact.

Silence.

What?

NOEL. I thought I'd let you say something. Yer go around as if everybody's about to criticise yer.

RHONA. They do.

NOEL. Yer determined to get in first.

A slight pause.

You know her friend.

RHONA. She has loads of friends.

NOEL. In France.

RHONA. Who?

NOEL. I thought you might know.

RHONA. Why should I?

NOEL. She needs a close friend around her.

RHONA. She's got me.

NOEL. We could write to her, if we had a mind to.

RHONA. I don't have a mind to. She can write herself, can't she? She's intelligent enough. She does write, anyway. Christmas an' that. Jamie told us.

NOEL. Will you think about it?

RHONA. No. Why should I?

A slight pause.

NOEL. Do you work, Rhona?

RHONA *shakes her head.*

RHONA. Our Luke said yer fancied us. Yer don't, do yer? He said yer'd fancy anything. He said yer fancied animals, even.

A short silence.

What?

NOEL. He's wrong.

A slight pause.

He's a crippled little bastard.

A slight pause.

What d'you want for the baby?

RHONA. Clothes yer mean?

NOEL. What d'you hope for?

RHONA. I don't know.

A slight pause.

I hope it's a boy. It'll be something that's mine.

RHONA *climbs down off the rail.*

Yer all right really. I don't mind yer too much. Don't get big-headed with it.

NOEL. I'll try my best.

RHONA *goes in.*

NOEL *rests his arms on the rail and looks out at the night.*

KAY *comes onto the balcony. She has a blanket around her shoulders.* NOEL *turns and sees her.* KAY *leans on the rail beside him.*

KAY. What did you do to go to prison?

NOEL. Robbery, I suppose you'd say. A warehouse stacked to the rafters with cigarettes. I understand, Kay. There's nothing puzzling about what I did either. I was involved in a crime. Kids don't get that. They think there's more to everything.

KAY. Rhona has problems.

NOEL. I know.

KAY. In any case, you asked her. You're just as bad.

NOEL. Have I been told off?

KAY. Mmm. You promised.

NOEL. Did I? I don't remember.

KAY. You more or less did.

NOEL. Yes, I'm sure you're right.

A slight pause.

KAY. What will Jamie get?

NOEL. It depends.

KAY. I'm hoping against hope he'll be out to see his child born. Am I wrong?

NOEL. It's down to the judge.

KAY. I wanted him to be sentenced this afternoon.

NOEL. I know. They don't do that nowadays. They wait for the psychiatric reports.

KAY. This has gone on for a year. I've spent so long waiting. Yesterday I'd have given anything to know the decision you were going to make on the jury.

A slight pause.

You're looking at me as if that's not the way it seems.

NOEL. I don't mean to. I haven't a clue what any of us should seem like at this second.

Scene Five

The shops. Three weeks later in April. Late evening.

The Red Lanterns chip shop is closed.

LUKE *comes running on. He throws a brick at the Red Lanterns' window. The glass smashes completely, almost seems to explode, and cascades to the ground.*

RHONA *comes on. He looks at her.*

LUKE. Four years.

RHONA. Are yer feelin' guilt ridden at last?

LUKE. There isn't an ounce of guilt in me, kid. I've just got rid of it.

RHONA. Yeh, like the way yer treat our mam.

LUKE. Me mam's soft in the brain box. She's a pill popper, but without the fun.

RHONA. Whose fault's that?

LUKE. Not mine.

RHONA. That's what you always say. Yer'll go to the grave without fault, you. Yer'll meet up with me mam. I hope she thumps yer one.

LUKE. Me mam won't go to heaven. There's no tranquillisers.

RHONA. Yer think you will?

LUKE. I don't believe in it anyway.

RHONA. Yer believe in nowt. She's going mad up there because of you.

LUKE. I thought yer didn't live there no more.

RHONA. I don't. I'm with Jamie's mam. She needs a friend around her.

LUKE. I'm with meself, kid.

RHONA. You always will be as far as I'm concerned.

LUKE. Me mam does me washing.

RHONA. I know. She told us. She's become a launderette.

LUKE. I talk to her then. I get her prescription.

RHONA. Yeh, an' yer nick half of them. It's why she's jittery.

LUKE. Yer think I'd do that to 'er?

RHONA. I know yer would. I've been round there. I've counted them in the bottle.

LUKE. It does her a favour.

RHONA. What favour's that when it's at home?

LUKE. I'm weaning her off them.

RHONA. You're cleverer than the doctor. That's all I can say.

A slight pause.

Yer've made a right mess now.

LUKE. Don't panic. They'll know it's not your precious Jamie. Yer been to see him yet, our lass?

RHONA *shakes her head.*

RHONA. I saw him in court this afternoon, from the distance. They won't let us see him.

LUKE. Is he not happy?

RHONA. He's very unhappy. He weren't wearing shoelaces, even to be sentenced. It's not right.

LUKE. He will go to heaven. He's a good lad.

RHONA. D'yer think he will kill himself, Luke?

LUKE. No chance.

RHONA. He says he will. He says it in nearly every letter to everybody.

LUKE. Yer always worry, our Rhona. Yer always have.

RHONA. One member of the family has to. They're saying all we're doing is making him worser. It applies to his mam as well. I reckon she's brilliant, but who am I to know? We waited outside the court 'til he was in the dock, so we could get a glimpse of 'im as we went in. We couldn't talk to him or anything. There was six police in there an' all, with big grins on their faces like a pay rise had happened. The one who led it was there to see what he got, the one who elbowed me in the face as Jamie was arrested and put in the van. Nowt was done about that complaint, far as I've heard. The judge listened to a bit of stuff, and said four years.

LUKE. Yer just depressed.

RHONA. Who is?

LUKE. You. You want to take care of yourself. Have a good time on a night.

RHONA. I do already. Some days.

LUKE. I should take you out.

RHONA. Will yer? The two of us? On our own. Nowhere noisy.

It starts snowing. The snowflakes are large and flutter in the still air.

LUKE *looks up.*

LUKE. It's fucking April and it's snowing.

He opens his mouth, and puts his hands in his leather jerkin.

If yer open yer mouth yer can eat it.

RHONA *moves and catches a few snowflakes.*

RHONA. Yer can catch them.

LUKE *grabs one. He looks at his palm.*

LUKE. They're like melting jewels, our kid. We can build a snowman before long.

AGNÈS COLLIN *enters. She is sixty-nine years old, quite tall and thin with a bony face and long fingers. She is wearing a winter coat and stout shoes. She has an umbrella which the snow is settling on.*

RHONA *sees* AGNÈS *first. She nods in* AGNÈS*' direction.* LUKE *turns.*

Are yer wantin' something special? Or are yer here for the party?

AGNÈS. Could you tell me which one of these blocks is Cleveland House? I cannot anywhere see any signs.

RHONA *points.*

RHONA. It's that one.

AGNÈS. Thank you very much.

AGNÈS *turns to go, but changes her mind and turns back.*

I am looking for Mademoiselle Tonnerre.

LUKE. You're a brave thing, I'll give yer that.

RHONA. Yeh, she does live here.

AGNÈS. Thank you so much. To hear it is like music.

RHONA. I'll go and get her.

RHONA *exits.*

AGNÈS. Is the girl going to go and find her for me?

LUKE. She was desperate to go to the toilet like. She has an illness in her bladder.

A slight pause.

AGNÈS. The weather, I expect it to be better tomorrow.

LUKE. Are yer clairvoyant?

AGNÈS. No, I do not think so, but it would be useful to know the future occasionally. Are you?

LUKE. Yer utterly strange.

AGNÈS. I do so hope not.

AGNÈS *looks at the broken window.*

Who did this?

LUKE. Some scum did it earlier.

AGNÈS. I am not an aggressive person, but you are.

LUKE. This place is dangerous for the likes of you and me.

AGNÈS. I did wonder to myself.

LUKE. Yer did right. Someone who hits someone old should be hit hard themselves, I reckon.

AGNÈS. I am not too old.

LUKE. Yer not in yer dotage then?

AGNÈS. I think you should answer me that question.

LUKE. I mean it, what I said. They're bloody scum. We should be proud of our old people. No one's bothered about them, except me.

AGNÈS. Do I like you? I cannot be sure.

LUKE. Yer know Mademoiselle Tonnerre then, d'yer? I mean, I think of her as Jamie's mam.

AGNÈS. Yes, I do, but not as much as I used to. Can I trust you?

LUKE. Yeh.

AGNÈS. I do not know if I can, when you break windows for no sensible reason.

LUKE. I did that? Yer off yer head. Did yer see us?

AGNÈS. It is a little guess of mine.

LUKE. Next time yer guess, guess right.

AGNÈS. It is good you are kind to older people, and so to me.

LUKE. I didn't do it. I've got more dignity than that, I've more self-worth. Don't get me wrong. I'm not saying I'm an angel.

He points at the broken glass.

This is mindless stuff, and I've got a mind.

AGNÈS. Yes.

LUKE. Why don't yer believe us?

AGNÈS. Some experience, but I do believe you now.

LUKE. It's what gets people, yer know. Being accused of all the rubbish they didn't do. If yer want to know why there's anger, that's it put in a nutshell.

AGNÈS. I understand.

LUKE. D'yer reckon you're the new Messiah, or something? Knowing about people like me.

AGNÈS. I so wish you would stop being aggressive. I have not harmed you.

LUKE. Yer really are something, you are.

AGNÈS. Am I given a compliment?

LUKE. Yeh, for the moment.

AGNÈS *offers her hand.* LUKE *shakes it.*

AGNÈS. The English way.

LUKE. What's that?

AGNÈS. In France there is a kiss or two. Do you know Jamie?

LUKE. Yeh, he's me best mate, he's inside.

AGNÈS. I know you cannot be Noel for some reason.

LUKE. Get out, 'course not. Yer can have a million reasons. Pick a larger number.

AGNÈS. Rhona? No.

LUKE. Yer an extraordinary elderly biddy, aren't yer.

AGNÈS. Do you know about the letter?

LUKE. Yeh. What letter?

AGNÈS. It is one way or the other.

LUKE. Not me.

RHONA *comes rushing on. She is out of breath.*

RHONA. Hold on. She's coming.

AGNÈS. Rhona?

LUKE. Yeh.

RHONA. She won't be long. She's finding her coat.

RHONA *goes towards* AGNÈS.

Don't tell 'er we went through piles of letters f'your address. She'll do me real bad if she hears.

LUKE. What have yer been up to, our kid?

RHONA. I'm getting help, for Jamie.

KAY *enters with* NOEL. KAY *sees* AGNÈS *and stops.*

KAY. It is you, Nan.

AGNÈS. My dear Catherine. I am so pleased.

A short silence.

LUKE. What's going on?

KAY *faints. She ends up flat on the snowy ground.*

RHONA. I put she kept on doing it.

AGNÈS. Yes, I see.

RHONA. It's about the seventh time she's fallen over.

KAY *starts to pick herself up.*

KAY. Is it you? Are you responsible? Who do I criticise?

NOEL. Yes, it was. I'm sorry.

KAY. You gave me your word. You promised.

RHONA. It was my idea like. I hunted around through all yer private stuff.

KAY. There is no money. Why don't both of you listen? It's gone. For pity's sake hear what I'm saying.

RHONA. I was trying to be kind.

KAY. I haven't the energy for all this.

RHONA. I thought you'd like it. I don't see much what I've done wrong.

KAY *and* AGNÈS *find themselves looking at one another.*

KAY. When you live here everything is about money. They think there's nothing else.

RHONA. Yer making it up.

KAY. Am I?

RHONA. Yeh, yer are. It's in your head. Yer going bonkers.

AGNÈS. You do not look at all well, Catherine.

KAY. That's right, Nan, always speak the truth. No matter how much it hurts anybody.

AGNÈS. I do not intent to be so hurtful. I did not imagine.

AGNÈS' *hand goes limp. The umbrella ends up pointing at the ground.*

LUKE. Were you her nanny?

AGNÈS. Yes.

LUKE. She likes yer really.

RHONA. It's more than she does me.

RHONA *takes the umbrella from* AGNÈS. *She holds it over her.*

AGNÈS. I had no idea. We were sometimes at cross purposes, as you used to say. It is not the time for us to have many recriminations. It is too long ago.

KAY *looks down.*

KAY. Yes.

AGNÈS. I have come from France today.

A slight pause.

When you stopped writing to me a few years ago I was offended.

KAY *looks up.*

KAY. You never ever had any rights over me, Nan.

A slight pause.

I was embarrassed.

AGNÈS. Why, Catherine?

KAY. Oh, I was embarrassed about Jamie.

RHONA. Is that your name, Kay?

KAY. Yes.

RHONA. Funny thing.

KAY *looks at* AGNÈS.

KAY. I was embarrassed about his getting into trouble. It's so silly.

RHONA. She's going to faint again.

KAY. I'm not. You were tough, but I never was. I was soft. I was quiet like my father. I was placid. Jamie is like his grandmother. He's as wilful as her. I've tried.

RHONA. He's not wilful.

KAY. He is.

RHONA. Trouble is, you don't like him much.

NOEL. Quiet, Rhona.

RHONA. Why should I be? It's my life. Jamie always said so.

NOEL. There's a time and a place.

A slight pause.

AGNÈS. I am staying in an hotel in the centre of the town, Catherine.

KAY. Yes.

AGNÈS. I can go there, and I can come back here tomorrow afternoon.

KAY. Yes.

AGNÈS. I would so enjoy being with you, but it must be your wish.

RHONA. She can stay with us, can't she?

KAY. Where?

RHONA. I don't mind sharing. I'm not bothered.

LUKE. You want to make up yer minds.

RHONA. I suppose you know what yer doin'?

LUKE. Yeh.

RHONA. Yer live in yer head.

LUKE. Indecision runs through yer like the plague, if yer let it.

AGNÈS. You are Luke.

LUKE. Told yer yer were a fortune teller.

AGNÈS. You are the bad apple.

LUKE. Don't know if I'm an apple.

AGNÈS. Let me just say that you are bad.

LUKE *stares at her.*

LUKE. You are going the right way about getting a smacking in the mouth.

KAY *rushes at* LUKE *and tries to slap him.* LUKE *is quick and fends her off easily. It happens so fast that it is hardly even a scuffle.* NOEL *tries to get between them, but* LUKE *ends up pushing* KAY *over.* LUKE *swings his foot to start to kick her.*

RHONA. Touch her and I'll never speak to you again.

Silence.

LUKE. All right, our lass, you win.

AGNÈS. I see how you got Jamie into all kinds of trouble, Luke.

LUKE. That don't include her.

RHONA. It does as far as I'm concerned. I'll go to the police. It's a promise.

LUKE. Yer growing up, our kid.

RHONA. Yeh.

LUKE. Don't grow too far.

RHONA. It won't be you who stops me.

LUKE *goes away to the Red Lanterns.*

NOEL *is beside* KAY *who is sitting on the snow. She has her head on her knees.* RHONA *bends down.*

NOEL. Well done Rhona.

RHONA. Thanks.

KAY *looks up.*

KAY. I'm sorry, Nan.

AGNÈS. No.

KAY. We squabble. It's all it is. It blows over.

AGNÈS. No.

KAY. It goes away.

AGNÈS. It is my fault. I was impatient to see you again.

KAY *gets up.* RHONA *holds the umbrella over her.*

Was I such an ogre when you were a child?

KAY. Sometimes.

AGNÈS. You did not tell me.

KAY. How could I.

AGNÈS. No.

KAY. You were not my mother.

AGNÈS. I did not want to be your mother.

KAY. You were not a mother to me. You did not do mothers' things.

AGNÈS. I wished for you to be happy so much. It was so difficult to know.

KAY. Yes.

AGNÈS. I tried to understand.

KAY. You did, but I wanted something more. None of it was enough. I needed you, Nan. I used to dream that you were my mother. That's how helpless I was. I always hoped you'd dream that I was your child. It's all so silly.

AGNÈS. Yes.

KAY. Did you ever?

AGNÈS. No.

A slight pause.

KAY. You see why I didn't want you to come here.

AGNÈS. Yes, Catherine.

KAY. Why I'm so embarrassed.

LUKE. She's called Kay. She was posh, eh? Once. Loaded with money. It's a bit of a come down this, isn't it. Jamie told us. Jamie told everyone what he thought, apart from his mam.

It stops snowing.

LUKE *runs his foot through the broken glass.*

D'yer know the only thing we share on this estate? I'm talking about emotional things. It's forgiveness. It's why the police daren't come here, because we forgive each other. An'

I'll tell yer this for nothing. Forgiveness in this instance is fucking despair.

KAY *is looking at him.*

You were great to me when I was this high to a grasshopper. I've never said, Catherine. I suppose I said when I was tiny in the cuddles I gave you. I've not forgotten. I used to steal them from Jamie, didn't I? Yeh, I was really envious. Dead jealous. I'm not the same as every loudmouth thug, who has a comment on everything and an insight into nothing. Yeh, I'm bad. But I'm not as bad as some.

KAY. Why, Luke?

LUKE. Why what? It's hard to say, isn't it. I've just been trying to as a matter-of-fact. It's the best I can do.

KAY. You could have come to me at any time.

LUKE. Could have. I couldn't. I wouldn't have kicked you by the way.

KAY. Wouldn't you?

LUKE. Only as a mistake. Yer get that it becomes a mistake. Sometimes I don't know the difference between love and making a big error. I know you loved us. Still do, maybe. I can hope, can't I? Yeh, that's weak. You weren't an idiot, Kay, so yer didn't bawl us out. I used to think of you as me dad, because I had a mam, and I was dadless. It's daft, isn't it? I used to think it'd be magnificent if you were me dad.

NOEL *takes hold of* KAY*'s hand.*

NOEL. We should go in.

KAY. In a minute.

LUKE. Yeh, I'm even jealous of you at this actual second. That's pathetic an' all. Don't be too shocked. This whole thing's got nowt to do with you. You don't belong on this estate, in these blocks.

NOEL. I'm not interested.

LUKE. Yer should be.

NOEL. I don't have to listen to you justify yourself.

LUKE. Yeh, yer right, yer don't. One day you'll break some news, until then keep off.

RHONA. Did yer really think of her as our dad, our kid?

LUKE. Yeh.

RHONA. Yer've never said before.

LUKE. It didn't matter before somehow.

RHONA. Why?

LUKE. It weren't relevant to anything.

RHONA. We had different dads anyway. So me mam says.

LUKE. She'd be the last person to know, our lass.

NOEL *touches* KAY*'s cheek.*

NOEL. Let's go in. Your friend must be cold. I've got to go home tonight.

RHONA. Where's your wife like?

NOEL. She's at her sisters playing Newmarket.

LUKE. Yer have a hobby, d'yer?

NOEL. I don't have to explain myself to you.

LUKE. I did.

RHONA. He did, yer know.

LUKE. Yer conscience ever prick yer?

NOEL. Yes. Sometimes.

LUKE. It doesn't stop you.

NOEL. No.

LUKE. What d'you call a hypocrite?

NOEL. I didn't put anyone in hospital. I didn't nearly kick someone to death.

LUKE. Round here we call them the police.

KAY. Stop it. Please stop it.

A slight pause.

LUKE. I don't know how you fell out. You two. If yer did fall out. But it seems daft to me, if I can have an opinion.

AGNÈS *bends over and puts her hands on her knees.*

AGNÈS. I think it is catching.

RHONA *furls the umbrella and goes to her. She puts her hand on* AGNÈS*' back.*

RHONA. You've got to take deep breaths.

AGNÈS. I will be better in a few moments.

She straightens up.

There you are. I told you.

LUKE. Yer really ace, you are. Give us a bit of time and I might even get to like yer.

RHONA. Yeh, he's right. He always is right.

AGNÈS. Thank you, Luke.

LUKE. Yer see things as they actually are. Yer like me. I do.

AGNÈS. Do I? I do not know if I do.

LUKE. Yer do it by mistake then. It comes down to the same.

AGNÈS. You do not know me, child.

LUKE. Yer get an instinct, don't yer.

AGNÈS. Perhaps.

KAY. Stop being manipulative, Luke.

LUKE. I'm not. It's the truth.

A slight pause.

AGNÈS. Well, I am here, and it has all been somewhat of a shock to see everyone.

A slight pause.

KAY. Would you like to come and stay with us?

AGNÈS. You must have more to think about than me.

KAY. Yes and no. No. It will mean mucking in.

AGNÈS. It is nearly twenty years, Kay. Well, I have tried to call you that.

KAY *smiles.*

KAY. We'll fit you in. We can squeeze you in somewhere.

AGNÈS. Thank you, I will. Not tonight.

KAY. It's more than twenty years, Nan. Jamie is twenty in August.

A slight pause.

RHONA. Yer can have Jamie's bed.

She looks at LUKE *for a second.*

I'm not like him. That's all yer need to know about me.

AGNÈS. I am very pleased to hear it.

LUKE. I thought yer liked us.

AGNÈS. Yes, I do. I genuinely do. Is that enough reassurance for you to be going on with?

LUKE. Yeh, it is.

LUKE *is embarrassed. He looks down and runs his foot over the broken glass.*

AGNÈS *looks at* KAY.

AGNÈS. You know, Catherine, I keep wanting to say how lovely it is to see you.

KAY. Say it.

AGNÈS. I just have.

LUKE. Yer should make up and have done with it.

AGNÈS. It is such a pity you do not do more with your life.

AGNÈS *holds out one of her hands.* KAY *goes to her and takes hold of both of her hands. They kiss on both cheeks.*

LUKE. I'm bloody freezing.

He blows on the backs of his hands.

I'm going to go in. See yer.

AGNÈS. I am grateful to you.

LUKE. Yer all right.

LUKE *runs off quickly.*

NOEL *joins* KAY *and* AGNÈS.

NOEL. Thank you for coming.

AGNÈS. It is a pleasure to be here. You must be Noel.

NOEL. Yes.

NOEL *and* AGNÈS *shake hands.*

I hope I'll meet you again.

He looks at KAY.

I'm going to go as well. Or I'll miss the last bus.

KAY. You don't have to.

NOEL. I should tonight.

AGNÈS. I may see you tomorrow, perhaps. I will look forward to it. I should be thanking you, not you me.

NOEL *touches* KAY*'s arm. He goes.*

RHONA. I'd better make myself scarce. Had I?

KAY. Don't be silly.

AGNÈS. I have a taxi waiting for me.

KAY. Will he stay for a few more minutes?

AGNÈS. I think so. He would not come as far as this.

KAY. No, they never will.

It starts snowing.

RHONA *walks away to the Red Lanterns.*

AGNÈS. He is remarkable.

KAY. Who?

AGNÈS. The young boy.

KAY. Luke.

AGNÈS. Yes, Kay. Well, I will keep on trying.

KAY. You don't have to.

KAY *touches* AGNÈS*' arm.*

He and Jamie used to play together. All the children would tear about between the various flats. They still do. They'd go in and out of each other's doors like they were one family. Most families got muddled up. He's forgotten. Once or twice he actually called me dad. I remember it vividly. He used to wait and seek me out when I was on my own.

KAY *touches* AGNÈS*' arm.*

It's good to see you. I was always awkward about touching, if you remember.

AGNÈS. Yes.

A slight pause.

KAY. He was so affectionate. I loved him for it. It's awful, isn't it?

AGNÈS. I am not quite sure what you are asking me?

KAY. Nothing. That I should have loved him more than Jamie, Nan. It's not wholly true.

AGNÈS. Yes, it is rather unfortunate.

A slight pause.

RHONA. Did you, honestly?

KAY. He was eight, I suppose, or nine. Certainly he was old enough to know what he was doing, Rhona. I used to love it when he'd turn up with his pyjamas in a bag. He needed me. We were kindred spirits.

RHONA. Didn't yer like Jamie?

KAY. Of course I did.

RHONA. Yer didn't.

KAY. Jamie was always steady.

RHONA. Yer should be sorry, you.

KAY. I am. I'm deeply sorry. I should never have had a child, Nan. It was a mistake, I remember you telling me. Only one of our many disagreements. It was our last argument, before I left for England. They were idiotic battles of wills. Of course I was wrong. I swopped the estate for a child. I got myself pregnant. I thought it would all come right.

KAY*'s hands are shaking. She runs her hands through her hair.*

I didn't know I'd end up here. I didn't know what it was to have nothing. Your mother was always inadequate. I did the best I could.

RHONA. She's dead in every way except she's alive, me mam.

KAY. Not once have you thanked me, Rhona. Not once. It's a bit much.

RHONA. I didn't know I had to like.

AGNÈS *goes to* KAY.

AGNÈS. Let me try to give you some energy.

KAY. No.

KAY *stops* AGNÈS *from taking hold of her.*

I don't want you, Agnès. I'm ill. I'm wound up so tight at the moment. I do love him, you know.

AGNÈS. Yes.

KAY. He doesn't want to see me. He blames me, I'm certain he does. I did try. I didn't succeed. I'm so frightened. I need you to help me.

AGNÈS. Yes.

AGNÈS *takes hold of* KAY.

A pause.

KAY. Thank you.

A slight pause.

Will you go and see him for me?

AGNÈS. I do not know how I will achieve it at this moment. Yes, I will.

KAY. He'd listen to you.

AGNÈS. I do not know why, my love.

KAY. It's what he needs. He needs you badly. He'd understand. I know he would. You're so much better than me.

AGNÈS. No. No.

AGNÈS *holds* KAY*'s head.*

I will try so very hard for you.

Scene Six

The shops. A short while later.

It has stopped snowing.

LUKE *is sitting on the rubbish bin. He jumps off.*

AGNÈS *enters.*

LUKE. Are yer going to stay with them?

AGNÈS. Yes. Tomorrow, as I explained.

LUKE. I saw yer go in. I was watching. I got rid of him for yer.

AGNÈS. Who?

LUKE. Noel what's his face.

AGNÈS. I am very tired.

LUKE. It's sorted out. Yer taxi's over there.

LUKE *points.*

Car headlights flash on and off, briefly lighting the shops.

He's with me. I'm watching him.

He takes a packet of cigarettes from his jerkin pocket and offers them to AGNÈS.

AGNÈS. No thank you.

LUKE. Yer reckon I'm not worth bothering with. Become a member of the club. Yer see it's why I have to bother about meself.

AGNÈS. I will talk to you, child, but not now.

AGNÈS *walks towards the car.* LUKE *takes hold of her hand and stops her.*

LUKE. You owe me a few minutes for the taxi.

AGNÈS. I owe you nothing as far as I know.

She pulls her hand away.

LUKE *scrunches up the cigarette packet and kicks it in an arc to the ground.*

LUKE. It was empty. Got no money.

AGNÈS. What is it?

LUKE. You're getting angry.

AGNÈS. It has been a long day for me. I would ask you to understand.

LUKE. Yeh, I do. Can yer make it a bit longer?

AGNÈS. Why must I?

LUKE. I need you. Yer can stay with me. I've got a flat.

AGNÈS. No.

LUKE. I thought you wouldn't.

A slight pause.

AGNÈS *looks down.*

They said, when I was at school, that I could dowse the flames of the devil.

AGNÈS *looks at him.*

AGNÈS. I do not doubt it for one second.

LUKE. In their impatience to get at me, they got it wrong. They meant the opposite. I've got a bed yer can have. I'll sleep on the floor.

AGNÈS. I am pleased to hear it.

LUKE. I'm clean.

AGNÈS. No.

LUKE. Yer won't be sorry. Yer only ever sorry about the things yer don't do. Yer thinking about it.

AGNÈS *smiles.*

AGNÈS. No.

LUKE. I bet you're evil sometimes.

AGNÈS. I am not as evil as you.

LUKE. There's time.

A slight pause.

AGNÈS. This is hopeless.

LUKE. What is?

AGNÈS. You are hopeless. The whole thing here. I cannot do this, child.

A slight pause.

LUKE. Shall I tell yer something? I've got a fucking hard-on.

A slight pause.

AGNÈS. I think we have said enough to each other.

LUKE. It happens to me when I get close to people. It's not sexual.

A slight pause.

AGNÈS. What do you want of me?

LUKE. To talk to you. Like we're doing.

AGNÈS. Why?

LUKE. I feel bad. Is that wrong?

AGNÈS. No. It is right.

LUKE. You're the first French person who's ever cared about me.

AGNÈS. Catherine cared.

LUKE. Yeh, she did. I'm talking about recently. I nearly love you.

AGNÈS *looks down.*

It's not sexual by the way. Me hard-on's gone off a bit. I think it was the first excitement, yer know.

AGNÈS. No.

LUKE. Yer do.

AGNÈS *looks up.*

You're the first French person who's taken me as I am. Before yer say owt, Kay did, but that's over. Yeh, I've hurt her really badly. Yeh, I wish I hadn't. Yeh, I wish I had more control than I'm showing yer. I wouldn't have told yer about me dick if I was sensible. Except you've not run off. I'd like to think I can be good, with your help. Will you help me, please?

A slight pause.

AGNÈS. I do not know if I can.

LUKE. Neither of us knows.

AGNÈS. I am not even slightly perfect.

LUKE. You are to me. Will you stay with us, please?

A slight pause.

AGNÈS. No, I will not do that.

LUKE. Can I go to France with yer, please?

A slight pause.

AGNÈS. We will have to see.

AGNÈS *puts one of her hands to the back of her neck and massages the tension that is there.*

I think I will have to ask Jamie.

LUKE. What about? What yer doing? Yer got a crick?

AGNÈS. Yes, something of the sort.

LUKE. I can rub it for you.

AGNÈS. No.

LUKE. I've magic hands.

AGNÈS. You make me nervous, a little.

LUKE. Why?

AGNÈS. Would you be prepared to make an arrangement?

LUKE. What's that?

AGNÈS. A deal, between us two.

LUKE. Yeh.

AGNÈS. I think we must do nothing without getting his permission first.

A slight pause.

LUKE. Get out.

AGNÈS. If he would like you to go to the police, child, then that is what you will do.

LUKE. I'd rather go to France.

AGNÈS. I think you must take me seriously, or leave.

A slight pause.

LUKE. You don't know what you're asking.

AGNÈS. I do.

LUKE *puts his hand gently onto her neck and massages it.*

LUKE. People are usually scared.

AGNÈS. I am.

LUKE. It's not sexual. It's affection.

AGNÈS. You are mixed up.

LUKE. Yer enjoying it really.

AGNÈS. No.

LUKE. This arrangement is going to be difficult.

AGNÈS. Yes.

AGNÈS *tilts her head back.* LUKE *puts his other hand onto her neck. He gently massages it with both hands.*

Silence.

He takes his hands away.

The lights of the taxi flash on and off.

LUKE. You were always safe.

AGNÈS. Why do you hate me?

LUKE. I don't. I love you.

AGNÈS. Do you know what love is?

LUKE. Not your sort. My own sort.

AGNÈS. Love is the same in every person.

LUKE. Is it?

AGNÈS. Yes.

LUKE *thinks.*

LUKE. I'll think some more.

A slight pause.

AGNÈS. I like you very much.

LUKE. Yer just sayin' it. I don't blame yer.

AGNÈS. We will see about France.

LUKE. Yer sound like Kay when I was tiny. When I used to go to her. Don't twist his arm, any how. Jamie's good. He don't deserve bad.

He picks up the cigarette packet and looks inside.

Yer can hope.

He throws it away again. He sits on the rubbish bin.

I'll sit here like a gnome while you disappear.

AGNÈS. You should see France, if Jamie wishes. You should see where Kay was brought up, and where I still live.

LUKE *shakes his head.*

LUKE. No. It's up to you.

AGNÈS. She gave me the cottage – it was a present – the home I have.

LUKE. Dead gracious of her, eh?

AGNÈS. Yes, it was.

LUKE. Jamie wanted to go, yer know. He told us lots of times.

A slight pause.

AGNÈS. Goodnight, Luke.

LUKE. Comment allez-vous?

AGNÈS. Très bien, merci.

LUKE. Kay taught us bits. I can't call yer Nan, can I? It'd be stupid.

AGNÈS. Yes. Agnès Collin.

LUKE. Agnès from France. See you around.

AGNÈS *goes to the taxi.*

The car drives off. Its headlights pass across the shops.

LUKE *watches the car go.*

The interval.

ACT TWO

Scene One

The visitor's room at Deerbolt Young Offenders' Institution. Two weeks later.

The walls are painted a bland, pale green colour which changes shade half way up. There is a door, and a high window which is letting in a shaft of sunlight. In the room is a metal trestle-table and two chairs. On the table is a tinfoil ashtray.

AGNÈS *is there, standing waiting.*

The door opens and JAMIE *comes in. He is wearing a blue, prison jumper and cotton trousers. He has his hands in his pockets to keep his trousers up. His shoelaces are missing. He shuts the door and stays by it.*

AGNÈS. Hello, Jamie.

JAMIE. Yeh, I know who you are.

He looks at the floor.

AGNÈS. I know you are innocent of this crime, but you were not so innocent all the other times, were you?

JAMIE. It's a great start to have.

A slight pause.

AGNÈS. I am sorry.

JAMIE *looks up.*

JAMIE. It's full of criminals. If yer like criminals it's brilliant.

He looks down.

AGNÈS. I hear you are too afraid to have a shower with the other boys.

JAMIE. Yeh, yer get raped and that's it. They banged us up. I knew that jury was against us from the beginning. I suppose yer better than mum. Anyone's better than her.

AGNÈS. Come over here.

JAMIE *goes to the table. One of his shoes comes off. He puts it back on. As he does so his trousers slip down an inch or two. He pulls them back up. He has yet to really look at her.*

AGNÈS *moves her fingers to his chin to lift his head up, but* JAMIE *pulls away.*

You know I wrote a letter to the Governor as well as to you.

JAMIE. Yeh.

AGNÈS. This visit is courtesy of him.

JAMIE. If you're tryin' to tell us they're shit paper soft, give up. It's what I get called. Personally I don't think it's very original.

He takes a packet of cigarettes from his trouser pocket. He keeps his other hand in his pocket to hold his trousers up. He lights one.

I don't want to see her. She makes it worse.

AGNÈS. Can you tell me why?

JAMIE. She's too good.

JAMIE *sits down.* AGNÈS *takes a packet of cigarettes from her coat pocket and puts them on the table in front of him.*

AGNÈS. I have never smoked, Jamie.

JAMIE. Thanks.

AGNÈS *sits down opposite him.*

AGNÈS. I think it must go back to when I was girl, to before the war when Germany was to come. My papa had a tin he used to put his tobacco money in to save for a piano. It is the only round tin I remember with a hinge on the lid.

JAMIE. How can yer have a hinge on something round?

AGNÈS. Well, it had a bevel at the top. A small flat surface you would hardly notice.

JAMIE *looks at her.*

JAMIE. Yer not like I thought yer'd be much.

AGNÈS. No? Which sort of person did you imagine?

JAMIE. I d'know. I'm not fussed, are you?

AGNÈS. I am interested to hear.

JAMIE. Can't say really. There's criminals everywhere yer turn. There's car crime, burglary, criminal damage, theft, deception, armed robbery, violence. Yer forced to mix with worse than worse. I'm classed as vulnerable.

AGNÈS. I know. I would be vulnerable too.

JAMIE. I don't mind you knowing for some reason.

A slight pause.

It's like having a song yer hate stuck inside yer head for five weeks. Yer can't just go to the pub to brighten yourself up.

AGNÈS. Yes.

JAMIE. The first day I thought I'd go to the pub tomorrow, but yer can't. There's no way out once yer in. That jury didn't listen to the evidence. They didn't sift through it. They can't have done, otherwise I'd be at home.

AGNÈS. I have spoken to your care officer just now.

JAMIE. Yeh.

AGNÈS. They are as sympathetic as it is possible for them to be.

JAMIE. No one cares.

AGNÈS. Well, as far as they are concerned you are guilty. You are not innocent in life, Jamie, are you?

JAMIE. I'm not even on F wing.

AGNÈS. What is that?

JAMIE. It's different. Yer get treated better. You could speak to them for us about going on F wing.

AGNÈS. I have no power to alter anything.

JAMIE. I want to go into Middlesbrough to get Rhona a ring. She's expecting the baby. Is it in November?

AGNÈS. I think your mum said the end of November.

JAMIE. Yeh. I'm looking forward to it. It'll be good. Yer can't stop yerself coming to prison. Yer come, don't yer? They send yer. I was busy doing my Community Service Order. I think the judge cancelled it, didn't he?

AGNÈS. Your mother will know.

JAMIE. I can't remember. I wasn't listening by then. I know he didn't like us. I didn't have anything with me even. I only had me clothes. I don't know if you're allowed to pack a bag or something, in case. You don't know what the jury's going to decide, do yer. After that yer've had it. You're straight here. No one says we'll think about it for a bit longer. It's not right. They don't think to ask you where you'd like to go. That's not right either. You should be given a choice. There should be brochures to look at. They should think what's best for the person, because you're the one doing the punishment.

AGNÈS *takes hold of his hand on the table.*

AGNÈS. Your mother is thinking about you all the time.

She takes the cigarettes.

I am going to open these. I can only give them to you if you are smoking them.

AGNÈS *unwraps the cellophane.*

JAMIE. I want to go home. It's never been my fault, all that's happened. You ask anybody. Everybody'll tell yer how I've always been unlucky with the police coming round. All it is, is I've been a target for some reason. I don't know why. I wish I did. I was the one, with mum, who tried to stop it. The police used to thank her at one time. People would come round and mum would make them tea. We had open house for problems. She used to listen to everybody. I'd come home from school and half the estate'd be in there. Yer'd come in and women would be crying. They're the mothers of the criminals. It's not me. I couldn't get in for crying for some days. I didn't do half what was read out in court. I was a target. It's not my work to do the police's job for them. They should go out and catch the criminals more.

His fingers are shaking. He puts out his cigarette.

Yer can get us out of here, can't yer?

AGNÈS. Well, I only wish I could.

JAMIE. I worked it out yer could. It's easy.

AGNÈS. How?

JAMIE. I was leaving it to you.

AGNÈS. No.

JAMIE. What's the point of yer coming then? Why did yer come?

JAMIE *gets up off the chair and walks towards the door. His trousers fall down. He stops.*

AGNÈS *goes to him. She lifts up his chin with her fingers.*

AGNÈS. I wish I was wise.

JAMIE. Is that all yer can say?

AGNÈS. Yes.

JAMIE. It's not much.

AGNÈS *unfastens a safety pin that is in place for a missing button on her blouse, and kneels down. She pulls up his trousers and secures them at the waist with the pin.*

They'll take that off us. I'm not allowed it.

AGNÈS *stands up.*

AGNÈS. Well, you can be wise for both of us. I do not want you to hurt yourself. Perhaps it is not possible.

JAMIE. What?

AGNÈS. I know you must tell me what is possible.

JAMIE. Why?

AGNÈS. I cannot do a thing. It is up to you. You can live like this, or you can choose not to live like this in the future. You must decide. My choice would be not to live like this, but I am not you.

She puts her hand on his cheek.

I have so much sympathy for you that I am telling you the truth. I do not know how good or bad that is of me. I do not care. It is time you did the same thing. I have listened to you bleat, but not for much longer. I have heard enough self-pity to last me for the day.

JAMIE *clenches his fists.*

If I were you I would not dare. Let Luke do the fighting for you, Jamie. I think he always has.

JAMIE. Yer don't insult a mate.

AGNÈS. He is some friend of yours. You are prepared to be in here for him. That would not be me, but it is your choice.

JAMIE. He's always stuck up for us.

AGNÈS. Yes, I see.

JAMIE. At school he stuck up for us when I was picked on because of mum.

AGNÈS. No. You were picked on because you were you. If you were picked on at all. I wonder if you were. You had Luke to go to.

A slight pause.

JAMIE. Piss off, eh. Get lost. Mum was right. Yer a shit.

AGNÈS. You are no better than me.

JAMIE *goes to the table. He sits down.*

AGNÈS *puts her hands in her coat pockets and hunches her shoulders.*

JAMIE. Are you cold?

AGNÈS. I am frightened.

She takes out a marble which she holds between her thumb and forefinger.

JAMIE. I've got some of them.

AGNÈS. I took it from a tin in your bedroom.

AGNÈS *holds the marble and runs it about her palm.*

JAMIE. Yer don't seem frightened.

AGNÈS. No. I am.

AGNÈS *goes to the table and sits down.* JAMIE *takes the marble from her. He puts it in his mouth.*

No.

JAMIE *gives her the marble. She puts it in her pocket.*

JAMIE. Did yer dad get the piano he wanted?

AGNÈS. Yes, eventually.

JAMIE. I know already. Mum said you used to play the piano sometimes, so yer must have had one at home to learn.

AGNÈS. Your mother was more interested in reading. She had a good singing voice.

JAMIE. Did she? There's a piano in here. I've seen it. Don't know if there's a choir. I knew that jury was going to say I was guilty. It was a foregone conclusion right from the start. It should have gone to the magistrates court, like the others. It didn't need a jury. It was simple. It shouldn't have gone to court in the first place. No one listens. They don't think about you. They're all selfish. They think about themselves.

JAMIE*'s hand is shaking. He takes a cigarette from the new packet and lights it.*

They're not the ones who are suffering. They can go home at night. I want to go to the pub. It's my right to go to the pub whenever I want. No one can stop me. It's not fair. It's the biggest miscarriage of justice ever. I don't know why it isn't all over the papers. It should be.

A slight pause.

You don't listen. Yer march in here like yer God. Tellin' me what to do. At least mum doesn't. I'd rather see her. She didn't listen, ever. She preferred Luke to me. I know she did. I'd come home and there'd be problems all over the place. Women weeping. They'd bring their babies. It was like a nursery. I hate babies because of that. It's not my fault. Mum was never as fond of me as their babies. It's not surprising I'm the way I am. I had to cope as best I could.

AGNÈS *takes hold of his hand.*

I've lost my freedom. I've lost my freedom to be treated differently. It's not fair at all.

AGNÈS. Luke will go to the police if you want him to.

JAMIE. Will he?

AGNÈS. I think so.

JAMIE. Is that what he said?

AGNÈS. Yes.

JAMIE. I'll believe it when I see it.

AGNÈS. He's made a promise. I do understand if you think his promises are like confetti.

JAMIE. I know now. Did yer come to tell me this?

AGNÈS. Yes.

JAMIE. Why didn't you tell me before?

AGNÈS. Because –

JAMIE. What?

AGNÈS. I had hoped to do something else first. I wanted to convince you that it was not worth being loyal to him.

JAMIE. Yer didn't.

AGNÈS. No. I failed. So I am doing it now.

JAMIE. Yer think I'm loyal to him?

AGNÈS. Yes.

JAMIE. I'm not. I don't like him much any more. He's not been to see me. I'm not a grass. There's prisoners in here get a biro and fasten a razor blade on the end of it. Yer get slashed. I've seen it. They don't even use the biro up first. And if they don't have a biro they use a toothbrush. That's what happens to you when you grass.

AGNÈS. No one is asking you to. Luke will go on his own.

JAMIE. Yer know something?

AGNÈS. No.

JAMIE. I feel dead sorry for you. Yer'll believe anything. Get lost.

JAMIE *gets up and goes to the door. He is about to open it when he changes his mind. He walks back to the table.*

I forgot me fags.

He puts them in his trouser pockets.

A slight pause.

He decides to sit down.

AGNÈS. Thank you for not walking off.

JAMIE. Actually, yer've made us feel better a bit.

AGNÈS. Have I?

JAMIE. Yeh.

A slight pause.

AGNÈS. Will you think about it?

JAMIE. I already have. Yer the lowest of the low. You've got to have your self-respect in here. If yer grassed they'd be on your case even more. The bully boys. I'd only be storing it up for the future. With violence yer get to the top of the pecking order. There's one prisoner in here. He's weak. I'll never be weak, if can help it. Some lads started messing about. I saw it with my own eyes. Flicking him with wet towels, punching him. Two of these three lads pinned him to the bed. The other one had a hypodermic needle. He pushed it through into his mouth –

JAMIE *touches his cheek.*

onto the gum and started to scrape his teeth with it. All he'd done was to shout out in his sleep. I don't even know what he'd shouted. Yer can't say anything or they'd be on your case. Yer see why I've got to get out. It's not fair. It's not civilised. It's too much punishment for what I did. Yer punished once, then yer punished again by everyone else who's in here. They should stop the bully boys. It should be against the law. It should be illegal to hurt another person. There needs to be tougher limits. It's not me who's wrecking things. I'm quiet. I'm in favour of the law. There's people being damaged by it all. There's victims. People should think about what their situation is. It's nobody's fault if they're a victim. There needs to be more sympathy. I'm in favour of the victim. I want to see people punished. I want to see them hurt more. It's not enough what goes on. It isn't according to the laid down rules. It's not honest.

JAMIE *gets up and goes to the door. He opens it.*

They're coming.

AGNÈS *gets up and goes to him. She closes the door.*

AGNÈS. I was promised an hour.

JAMIE. You were going to get us out. Yer haven't done yet. I don't know why yer bothered. I don't know why I bothered. It's a waste of time. I could be busy.

AGNÈS. Jamie, stop it.

JAMIE. What?

AGNÈS. Please stop it.

JAMIE. What've I got to stop? Tell us and I will.

AGNÈS. I have feelings, too. Yes, Jamie? If I had some magic I would use it. I am not a punch-bag to be treated any how you choose.

AGNÈS *looks down.*

Well, I am not accusing you.

JAMIE. What d'you want?

AGNÈS *looks up. She runs her hand up and down his arm.*

AGNÈS. You had better go. It is wrong to keep you.

JAMIE. You don't know me. Yer not family. It's nothing to do with you.

AGNÈS. Yes.

Silence.

JAMIE. Is this how you were with mum?

AGNÈS. Ask me that again?

JAMIE. Is this how yer were with mum? A lot like this, sometimes. She said you argued to the point where you were both silent for days.

AGNÈS. Yes, she is absolutely right. We did. Whenever I was wrong.

JAMIE. What did yer do?

AGNÈS. I interfered in her life in the wrong way, like now with you. I was meddlesome, always have been, and silly. One day I was her mother, not a friend. The next day I was a friend once more, not a mother. I was in the middle when the middle was no good.

JAMIE. She likes you.

AGNÈS *smiles.* JAMIE *shrugs.*

We don't know each other to know.

AGNÈS. Isn't it much easier to be honest with a stranger? There is nothing to lose. I think we have something that could be lost, you and me. What do you think?

JAMIE. Yeh.

AGNÈS. We have something to keep.

A slight pause.

You know, the best kind of loyalty is the loyalty you make a decision about.

JAMIE. Yer off again.

AGNÈS. Yes. It is not something you should drift into. It is seen as a virtue. It is not always so. I was loyal to your grandmother – she paid my wages and I did what she wanted most of the time – when I should have been loyal to your mother and her wishes. Your mother needed me. Your grandmother did not. I should have told her to get lost. I understand why you say it. It has taken me a long time to find the right sort of courage. That sort. Well, we all make mistakes.

A slight pause.

JAMIE. Yeh.

A slight pause.

AGNÈS. Luke wants to see where I live, in France. I said I would talk to you about it.

JAMIE. Why?

AGNÈS. It concerns you. Why should he be happy?

JAMIE. I've not been. I've never seen where mum grew up.

AGNÈS. I know.

JAMIE. Yeh, if yer want. I'm not fussed. It's not up to me.

AGNÈS. It is up to you. It is your decision.

JAMIE. Why?

AGNÈS. He owes you it.

JAMIE. I've said I don't mind.

AGNÈS. You should mind.

JAMIE. Yeh, he can go if he wants. I don't care.

A slight pause.

Why d'yer like us?

AGNÈS *shrugs.*

AGNÈS. Well, who knows.

JAMIE. Do yer like me?

AGNÈS. Very much.

JAMIE. Thanks.

JAMIE *opens the door.* AGNÈS *watches him go out.*

Scene Two

An unused storage room in the château in France. An afternoon in June.

The room is large and has been left untouched for a long time. The untreated stone walls are dry and dusty rather than damp. A series of circular windows, in the sloping roof, let in parallel shafts of natural light. Out of place, in one corner, is a lavatory and cistern, and a porcelain washbasin. At the other side of the room is a chest of drawers. Apart from these things the room is empty.

The oak door swings open and LUKE *enters. He is wearing a white teeshirt and has his jumper fastened around his waist. He looks about.* NOEL *enters.* LUKE *wanders to the lavatory and finds an empty champagne bottle in the bowl.* NOEL *ambles to the door, but* RHONA *comes in, and this stops him going out.* LUKE *blows across the top of the bottle making a note of sorts.* KAY *enters. She is wearing a skirt and a blouse.* NOEL *takes hold of her hand.* RHONA *goes to the lavatory, looks at it, and sits down on the edge.* KAY *looks at the ceiling.* AGNÈS *enters.*

LUKE *blows and makes a better note.* KAY *frees her hand and goes to the chest of drawers. She turns to look into the room.* RHONA *stands up.* LUKE *turns on one of the taps on the washbasin. Nothing comes out. He walks away.* RHONA *turns it off.* LUKE *ambles out of the room.* AGNÈS *wanders to the lavatory and pulls the chain. Nothing happens.* RHONA *exits.* NOEL *goes to* KAY. KAY *smiles and wanders to the washbasin.* NOEL *exits.* KAY *runs her fingers along the porcelain.* LUKE *wanders back in.*

LUKE. It's stupid having those. You can't have a toilet in a big room. You wouldn't catch me using it. I'd die first. I knew the French were funny about toilets the minute I got here.

He blows across the top of the bottle.

Aren't yer coming? Yer so slow. I can see stuff in half the time.

KAY. Don't be in such a rush. There's all afternoon to go at yet.

LUKE. You can remember it. I can't. It's all right for you. It means something.

AGNÈS. It's as simple as this – the boy has no imagination, Kay.

LUKE. What's that supposed to be about when it's at home? If it's a put-down, it's failed already. It doesn't even work all that, so what's the point.

He goes to a washbasin and turns on a tap. Water comes out.

It's not my fault. I can only say what I see.

AGNÈS *pulls the chain. The toilet flushes.*

KAY *wanders out of the room.*

Where's she going?

AGNÈS *turns off the tap.*

Is something going on here that I don't know about? I bet there is. Yer up to something, aren't yer?

AGNÈS *goes to the chest of drawers. She takes out a long, monk-like cassock that is on a hanger and wrapped in cellophane.*

AGNÈS. Yes, if you must know.

LUKE. Get out. What've I done wrong suddenly. I thought I'd been dead good.

AGNÈS. Well, you have been very good, but not quite good enough. I am only making a joke, Luke.

LUKE. Get lost, eh.

AGNÈS. No. I thought you liked a joke.

LUKE. I like me own jokes, me.

AGNÈS. Exactly so.

LUKE. I want to be buried beside you, so we can both have a laugh. Yer brilliant, you are. I'm never going to forget you.

LUKE *takes out a packet of cigarettes.*

AGNÈS. No smoking in here.

LUKE. Why?

AGNÈS. It was not allowed by Kay's mother.

LUKE. That was was, weren't it. Kay doesn't smoke anyway. It wasn't much of a loss.

KAY *takes the cassock out of its cellophane wrapping.* LUKE *puts away his cigarettes.*

Have you been fibbing to us?

AGNÈS. Fibbing?

LUKE. Pull the other one. You know what fibbing is as well as I do. Someone's been to the dry cleaners.

AGNÈS. Yes, it was musty with age, unlike me.

AGNÈS *goes to* LUKE. *She holds the cassock beside him.*

It will fit you.

LUKE. Yer'll be telling me next it was Kay's.

AGNÈS. I do not need to now.

LUKE. No one calls me daft, Agnès.

AGNÈS. I would never think you were daft, child. Put it on. Please, for me.

LUKE. Get lost. What for? It isn't fair, yer know.

AGNÈS. It is.

LUKE *begins to put on the cassock.* AGNÈS *helps him put it on over his head. The cassock covers him from his neck to his toes.*

LUKE. I bet I look like a monk, don't I?

AGNÈS. Yes, you do, which is surprising.

LUKE. I'm not in a good mood, yer know.

AGNÈS. Yes, you are. I admire the mood you have been in.

AGNÈS *pulls the strings together at the neck.*

You know you like nothing more than being the centre of attention.

She ties them loosely in a bow.

LUKE. It's great. It's absolutely the best. I could live here with you. Can I?

AGNÈS. Shoes and socks.

LUKE. What?

AGNÈS. Shoes and socks. Please, Luke, for me.

LUKE *takes off one shoe and one white sock. He undoes the other shoe and kicks it off across the room. He takes off the other sock.*

Teeshirt.

LUKE. I know where this is leading, yer know. I might not have sat exams. It didn't mean I couldn't.

He hitches up the cassock.

AGNÈS. Under the cassock.

LUKE *unfastens his jumper and drops it. He lets the cassock fall.*

LUKE. How?

AGNÈS. I undressed Kay when she was little. Bring one hand out of the neck.

LUKE *does so.*

Pull the teeshirt up at the back and bring it over your head.

LUKE *tries.* AGNÈS *helps him.*

Why are you so hopeless, child?

LUKE. I'm not.

AGNÈS. God gave you a brain to think about what you are doing.

LUKE. I missed out when God was around.

AGNÈS. Concentrate, for goodness sake.

LUKE. Don't get ratty.

AGNÈS. You are useless.

The teeshirt is off. LUKE *brings it out of the top of the cassock. He drops it.*

Pick it up and fold it, properly and neatly.

LUKE *looks at her. He picks up the teeshirt. He folds it.*

LUKE. What was this place anyway? It's not normal.

AGNÈS. Please stop talking.

LUKE. Can't smoke. Can't talk. Yer didn't have much fun.

AGNÈS. Jeans.

LUKE. I bet I look a right idiot. I feel like one.

AGNÈS. I will not ask you again, child.

LUKE. Don't blame me for nothing. I voted for a good time.

There is movement under the cassock. LUKE *steps to one side. His jeans are in a heap on the floor.*

AGNÈS *looks at him.*

You're not having owt else. I'll tell you that for free.

AGNÈS. Still you have not learnt.

LUKE. Learnt what?

AGNÈS. To take care of your things.

LUKE *picks up his jeans. He folds them. He puts them on top of the teeshirt.*

AGNÈS *picks up the shoe.*

Hold out your hands.

LUKE. Yer must be joking, aren't yer?

AGNÈS. Do as you are told for once.

KAY *wanders into the room.*

LUKE. Are you in on this an' all?

KAY. That's enough, Nan. It's plenty.

AGNÈS. He has to learn.

LUKE. Is the others? I wouldn't put it past them. Is our sister?

KAY *shakes her head.*

KAY. No.

AGNÈS. Give me your hands, child.

LUKE *holds out his hands.*

LUKE. Touch me and I'll whack you one back.

AGNÈS *crashes the shoe across one of his hands.*

KAY. Stop it. It's gone too far.

LUKE *is so shocked that he does almost nothing.*

LUKE. Jesus Christ that bloody hurts.

He shakes his fingers.

AGNÈS *crashes the shoe across his other hand.*

Ow.

LUKE *stares at her.*

AGNÈS. You do not touch me, child, ever. Is that perfectly clear?

LUKE. Yer didn't have to hit us.

LUKE*'s fingers are shaking. He rubs them together, gingerly. He blows onto them.*

AGNÈS. Get washed.

LUKE. Yer what? Yer must be eccentric. How?

AGNÈS. Are you an imbecile who needs to be told everything?

LUKE. No.

AGNÈS. Beneath the cassock.

LUKE. Keep yer hair on.

He goes to the washbasin.

What do I use?

AGNÈS. What is there.

LUKE. I can't see anything like.

AGNÈS. Use your hands.

LUKE. My hands hurt as matter-of-fact.

AGNÈS *goes to him. She turns on a tap.*

Yer stranger than bonkers, you are.

AGNÈS *takes hold of his fingers. She puts them under the water.*

I'm surprised yer not in a home for the funny.

LUKE *puts his hand inside the cassock, through the neck. He washes himself.*

KAY *goes to him.*

KAY. Come here.

LUKE *brings his hand out of the cassock.* KAY *takes it. She rubs his fingers. She looks at* AGNÈS.

No more. It's the finish.

LUKE. Is this what you did? Did you have to do this?

KAY. Yes.

KAY *starts to take off the cassock.*

LUKE. I'm only in me undies. It's rude.

KAY. I saw you in your undies often enough when you were little.

LUKE. I'm bigger now.

KAY. I'll cope.

LUKE *is wearing boxer shorts.*

AGNÈS *wanders to the door.*

LUKE. Yer don't have to go. I'm not embarrassed or owt.

AGNÈS *goes out.*

What for? Why did you have to do this? You were little then, weren't you.

KAY. I don't know what for.

KAY *holds his hands. She rubs his fingers.*

Is that any better?

LUKE. A bit. She really hit us. I didn't think she would.

KAY. If it's any consolation, she'll be upset.

LUKE. Will she?

KAY. Yes.

LUKE. It isn't much. Why?

KAY. She likes you. It's very simple.

LUKE. I don't get any of this. It isn't fair. Yer can't go around hitting people for no purpose. I'm a casualty, I am. It's all right for you, you're not. I suppose you are actually, in some ways. You're lucky, you've grown up. Jamie's the casualty. Is that what this about? Don't tell me. I've worked it out.

KAY *puts the plug in the basin and holds his hands in the water.*

Can I ask yer something, Kay? Was yer mam soft in the head? Don't tell me. I know she was. Our mam's brain dead. Most women are batty. I think I'll be gay from now on. Was she jealous, or something like that? Is it why she made yer do this? Who was she jealous of? Was she jealous of you?

KAY. Yes.

LUKE. Why? Don't tell me. Men are never jealous like women are jealous. I'll think I'll definitely be a pervy pouf the next time I fancy someone. Was she jealous because of yer dad? Because yer loved him a lot, and she knew that, I reckon. Yer dad left you all the money. I'd be jealous, so it must be the case. How could she do this to yer? How could she do this to a child? It's very wrong, I think.

KAY. Is the water helping?

LUKE. Not really.

KAY *smiles and kisses him on the forehead.*

I hate it when you do that.

KAY. Why?

LUKE. I hate it when you love me.

KAY *pulls out the plug.*

Can I ask yer something else, Kay? Don't tell me because I know. Did Agnès do what yer mam wanted? There's a story in here somewhere, I can tell yer.

KAY. That's the point, Luke.

LUKE. What?

KAY. That's what she wants you to see.

LUKE. She wants me to go to the police, more like. It's why all this goes deep.

KAY. She doesn't. She wants you to see there's a story.

LUKE. What story? Don't tell me.

LUKE *thinks for a long time.*

Did you do this every day?

KAY. Yes, when I was a girl, and throughout my teens.

LUKE *thinks.*

LUKE. Yeh, I see what yer mean a bit. It's bloody awful, isn't it.

KAY. You've got it. Yes. Has the penny dropped?

LUKE *thinks for a long time.*

LUKE. I don't know. It might have done.

LUKE *thinks.*

Can I ask you a daft question?

KAY. Whatever you like?

LUKE. Is it because I'm a self-centred slob?

KAY. Yes.

LUKE. Why d'you love me then?

KAY. Because I do.

LUKE *thinks.*

LUKE. You could say that was another story, couldn't you?

KAY. Yes, you could.

LUKE. There's stories everywhere, if you think about it like that.

LUKE *thinks.*

I see what yer mean. I see what she means an' all. Thank God I didn't belt her one. Funnily enough, yer know, I never felt like it. Why didn't I? It's dead important I know immediately.

KAY. She cares.

LUKE *thinks.*

LUKE. Yeh, yer right.

A slight pause.

Phew. I feel floppy.

KAY *smiles.*

What?

KAY. Nothing. I can smile.

LUKE. I am, I'm all floppy. I'm like a puppet.

He acts like a puppet for a brief moment, before he embarrasses himself.

Thanks for being me dad sometimes.

KAY. Don't go soft on me.

LUKE. I have to. It's the only way.

He thinks.

Can I ask yer something else? Don't tell me. Have I got a story? I have, haven't I? I need you to tell me, Kay.

KAY. Yes.

LUKE. If I know I've got a story, and it's still going on, then I can be in charge of it. Can't I?

KAY. Yes.

A slight pause.

LUKE. Yer saying I should think more.

KAY. Not just that.

LUKE. I've thousands of stories, come to think of it. Is the good story about to start?

KAY. Yes.

A slight pause.

LUKE. Phew. I'm floppy at the moment.

Scene Three

The room in the château. That evening.

Moonlight is coming in through the windows in the roof, lighting the room in a series of shafts.

LUKE *is sitting on the floor. He is wearing the cassock.*

AGNÈS *enters through the open door.*

LUKE. It's brilliant in here. I want to live in this place forever. Can I?

AGNÈS. It is time to come out. We are about to have dinner.

LUKE. I've never been less hungry in me life.

AGNÈS. If you live on thin air you will shrink.

LUKE. I won't. Talk French to us.

AGNÈS. Why?

LUKE. I like it.

AGNÈS. Non.

LUKE. You're shyer than yer pretend. I bet yer like yer own company more than you let on.

LUKE *gets up.*

Did you talk French to Kay?

AGNÈS. When?

LUKE. You know when. Ages ago.

AGNÈS. French and English. Mostly English.

LUKE. Pourquoi?

AGNÈS. Her mother insisted on it.

LUKE. Did yer carry out her orders?

AGNÈS. I had much to learn, the same as you.

LUKE. It's a dungeon this place. It's great.

AGNÈS. Put your things on now.

LUKE. You are beautiful when yer get bossy. Yer beautiful anyhow. Yer sexy.

AGNÈS. No, I am not.

LUKE. You are.

LUKE *takes off the cassock.*

Do I have to fold it?

AGNÈS. Throw it away.

LUKE. I'll never hurt you, ever.

LUKE *drops the cassock. He picks up his teeshirt.*

AGNÈS. I do not know, Luke.

LUKE. What don't yer know?

AGNÈS. I don't know much about much.

LUKE. Liar.

AGNÈS. I know a little about a little.

LUKE. Fibber.

LUKE *puts on his teeshirt. He picks up his socks and puts those on.*

AGNÈS. And even less about sex.

LUKE. I'm not sure about that like. I'll tell yer eventually.

AGNÈS. I live alone.

LUKE. So do I. I've learnt a thing or two.

AGNÈS. You are young.

LUKE. Don't give me that crap. I don't care. You don't if you're honest.

AGNÈS. I am very rarely honest.

LUKE. Absolute liar.

AGNÈS. Sometimes.

LUKE. No. Always.

LUKE *puts on his jeans.*

AGNÈS. Not always in the past.

LUKE. I'm talking about now. Today. This second.

AGNÈS. Yes.

LUKE. Yes what?

AGNÈS. Just yes.

AGNÈS *goes across the room and picks up the shoe.* LUKE *sits down. He puts on the shoe that is near him.* AGNÈS *gives him the other one.*

We should go.

LUKE. Yer didn't come to go.

AGNÈS. I did.

LUKE *fastens his laces. He stands up.*

LUKE. Why are you helping us, Mademoiselle Collin?

AGNÈS. Because you asked me to, child.

AGNÈS *runs her hand across his cheek.* LUKE *takes hold of her wrist.* AGNÈS *resists, up to a point fights back with strength of her own.* LUKE *takes* AGNÈS*' hand and pushes it down to between his legs.*

LUKE. Are you helping us now?

AGNÈS. I do not suppose so.

LUKE. Yer are. Are yer doing this for Jamie?

AGNÈS. No. For you.

LUKE *takes his other hand to the back of her neck.*

LUKE. Liar. Cheat. Deceiver. Lurker. Inventor. Lecher. I'm running out of them.

AGNÈS. I know I am doing this for me.

AGNÈS *kisses him. They kiss.*

LUKE. Why d'you live alone, Agnès Collin.

AGNÈS. It is easier.

LUKE. No.

AGNÈS. Fear.

LUKE. That's more like it. It's a pity yer too old to have my baby.

AGNÈS *smiles.*

What's funny about that? I mean it. You'd be a good mother.

AGNÈS. No. No.

LUKE. Pourquoi?

AGNÈS. I tried it once with Catherine.

LUKE. She wasn't yours.

AGNÈS. I know.

LUKE. Yer've either been promiscuous, you, or not promiscuous. I can't make up me mind.

AGNÈS. I have been very ordinary.

LUKE. Not ordinary. Why d'yer fancy us?

AGNÈS. I should not.

LUKE. It's not sympathy.

AGNÈS. No.

LUKE. It's something else. I can take it.

AGNÈS. You are bright.

LUKE. No, I'm not. I'm dead bright, me.

AGNÈS. A kind of empathy.

LUKE *takes hold of* AGNÈS *hand and puts it between his legs.*

LUKE. What's that?

AGNÈS. As you say, it is different from sympathy.

AGNÈS *moves her hand to the back of his neck.*

I was pregnant once but the baby was miscarried. Even Catherine does not know. She was about thirteen.

LUKE. This is a good place.

AGNÈS. No, not here.

LUKE. Pourquoi?

AGNÈS. Do you like the sound of that word?

LUKE. Yeh, love it.

AGNÈS. It has too many bad memories.

LUKE. Why didn't yer marry the guy?

AGNÈS. He did not love me. He was a doctor in Châlons-Sur-Marne. I think so.

LUKE. Aren't yer sure?

AGNÈS. I was at the time, thirty years ago.

RHONA *enters. She is carrying a large wooden tray which is stacked with plates, cutlery, glasses and two bottles of red wine.*

AGNÈS *and* LUKE *part immediately.*

RHONA. What're yer doing down here any road? We've been waiting ages and ages. Everyone's starving hungry.

AGNÈS. We were just coming now.

RHONA. Yer a bit late. We've already come to you.

KAY *enters with a bread basket and a bowl of salad.*

Where shall I put it?

KAY. Put it on the floor somewhere. Find a clean space.

RHONA. None of it's clean. It's all dusty. It's so mucky it'd still be mucky if you swept it.

RHONA *puts the tray on the floor.*

NOEL *enters. He is carrying a large metal casserole dish with a pair of oven gloves.* KAY *puts the bread basket on the lid.*

NOEL. This is still piping hot.

KAY *turns on the switch by the door. The electric wall lights come on.* NOEL *puts the casserole by the tray. He begins to sort out the glasses and wine.*

AGNÈS. We were coming.

KAY. It doesn't matter. It'll make a change.

NOEL. Who's for a drop of wine? Everyone? Rhona?

RHONA. Yes, please.

RHONA *is looking at the lavatory.*

It's convenient, but it's an odd place to put something like that. I thought it earlier.

KAY *puts the salad bowl on the floor.*

NOEL. Agnès?

NOEL *gives* AGNÈS *a glass of wine.*

AGNÈS. Thank you.

KAY *is sorting out the things on the tray.*

KAY. The lager's in short supply, Luke. We've run out. We'll have to get some more tomorrow.

NOEL *gives* RHONA *a glass of wine.*

RHONA. It's great this stuff. It tastes better than it does at home.

NOEL *gives* LUKE *a glass.*

NOEL. We missed you this afternoon.

LUKE. I'm sure you didn't.

NOEL. We did. Rhona and me went for a long walk.

LUKE. Where did you go?

NOEL. Across the fields towards Épernay, through some bullocks, down a bit to the river, and came back through the vines. Rhona got chatted up.

RHONA. I didn't.

NOEL. You would have done if his English had been better.

RHONA. He didn't let us know he was chatting us up. Was he?

LUKE. Who by?

NOEL. I'm only joking. One of the young blokes on the estate. I think he was helping his father, pushing the wheelbarrow.

RHONA. He was a schoolboy for a start. I've got more beard than him. He wasn't gorgeous.

KAY *is dishing up the chicken casserole.*

NOEL. It was delightful, Agnès. We got as far as Châtillon-sur-Marne before turning round. Some of the countryside is lovely. Especially the river and the trout. I don't know if you walk that way yourself ever?

AGNÈS. I go to Château-Thierry sometimes to see an old friend.

RHONA. We were looking for a shop to get some champagne. Weren't we?

NOEL. Yes.

RHONA. We couldn't find one. All this champagne stuff about and none to buy. It's daft.

AGNÈS. I know who you were talking to.

RHONA. Have I gone and put me foot badly in it?

AGNÈS. No.

RHONA. It wouldn't be the first time.

AGNÈS. He is the grandson of the owners, back from school. His English should have been better, since I taught him when he was a small boy.

RHONA. It was me shoutin' me bits of French at him. Perhaps he's more gorgeous than I thought. Was he really chatting us up?

NOEL. I don't know.

RHONA. Yer said he was. I reckon he was now yer say it. D'yer think I've ruined me chances?

LUKE. Rhona.

RHONA. What?

LUKE. Shut up.

RHONA. Why? What've I done wrong suddenly?

LUKE. Yer about to do wrong.

RHONA. That's good coming from you. I can fancy who I like. You always have. I couldn't marry him anyway because of you. Who wants a criminal in the family? You're the hindrance.

KAY. Come on everyone, before it starts to go cold.

AGNÈS *bends down.*

AGNÈS. What is there to do?

KAY. I've almost finished. Sit down, Nan. We'll have to eat off our knees.

AGNÈS *sits.* NOEL *and* RHONA *sit down.* KAY *gives them a plate of chicken casserole each, and they take their own cutlery off the tray.*

You have this one.

AGNÈS. That is far too much. Give me something smaller.

LUKE. I'll have it.

AGNÈS *gives the plate to* LUKE. LUKE *sits.*

KAY. There's some salad and some bread. I haven't dressed the salad. There's some olive oil somewhere.

RHONA. I don't like oil, and I don't like olives. It tastes like oil and olives to me.

They eat and drink wine.

LUKE. Who cooked it?

KAY. It was a joint effort.

AGNÈS. Catherine did the thinking. I chopped the vegetables.

LUKE. It's brilliant.

A slight pause.

NOEL. Did you teach, Agnès?

AGNÈS. Well, I used to teach the boy privately. It was not really arranged, he just used to come and see me. In return I was given little bits of things for the cottage. Especially some furniture I wanted.

KAY. You did teach, Nan.

AGNÈS. Yes, I was a teacher for twenty-one years, then I retired.

RHONA. What did yer teach?

AGNÈS. English.

RHONA. Where?

AGNÈS. In Reims, in a secondary school. I taught children their school certificate. I don't know what you call it in England any more. Is it GCSE?

RHONA. It's no good asking me. I didn't go if I could manage not to.

AGNÈS. I think it is.

NOEL. It is. My grandchildren are at school.

RHONA. Are you a granddad?

NOEL. Yeh.

RHONA. You don't seem like it.

KAY. Do I seem like a grandmother?

RHONA. No, come to think of it.

NOEL. Did you enjoy teaching?

AGNÈS. Well, I did, yes. It was hard work sometimes, and I struggled with some of the less able children. I don't know really. I should have had more patience.

KAY. You were a very good teacher.

LUKE. I bet you were ace.

AGNÈS. No, unfortunately. I should have been more tolerant. I didn't listen to people as I should have done. Listening is an art, you know. I think so.

RHONA. Eat up.

AGNÈS. Yes, I will.

AGNÈS *picks up the bread basket and hands it round. They help themselves to bread.*

NOEL. I'd liked to have become a teacher.

AGNÈS. Would you?

NOEL. Yeh. Done some good possibly, here and there.

LUKE. I would.

RHONA. You've more chance of dancing on the moon.

LUKE. I know.

NOEL. You had the countryside to walk across. You probably thought too much. I'm sorry, that was ridiculous.

AGNÈS. No.

NOEL. Do local people fish for the trout?

AGNÈS. Yes. The children mainly. The men and women who work here, their children. It is still like a family, you know, which it never was in Catherine's time. Please excuse me.

AGNÈS *stands up.*

I am going to go for a walk.

KAY. Shall I come with you, Nan?

AGNÈS. No. A shortish walk.

AGNÈS *goes out.*

RHONA. What have I done wrong?

KAY. Nothing.

RHONA. She's put me off me tea now.

NOEL. It's my fault. I shouldn't have gone dragging up the past.

KAY. It's nobody's fault.

LUKE *gets up and goes out of the room.*

RHONA. Where's he going? I might have known he'd have something to do with it. Yer can't eat a meal in peace with him around. I'll go. He'll only make her worse.

RHONA *starts to get up.*

KAY. Forget it, Rhona. Leave them be.

RHONA. I wrote to her. I'm responsible.

KAY. I know.

RHONA. She's supposed to be helping Jamie. I don't see much of it. All she does is talk to our brother.

KAY. What for?

RHONA. You tell me.

KAY. No. You tell me.

RHONA. I don't know.

KAY. She is doing what she can, which is more than you.

RHONA *looks down. She flicks some gravy off her plate with her knife.*

RHONA. Anyone would think I wasn't suffering. I don't have a boyfriend no more. I'm having a baby but no one's bothered.

LUKE *comes through the door.*

KAY. Is she all right?

LUKE. Yes.

LUKE *sits down.*

Everyone has to get on with their dinners.

LUKE *picks up the salad bowl and passes it to* NOEL.

NOEL. Thanks.

NOEL *helps himself to some salad.*

KAY. I'm sorry.

RHONA. Yer should be. You got pregnant when you weren't married. I don't criticise anybody. Who was he anyhow when he's at home?

KAY. His father was one of the workers.

RHONA. Was he a boy?

KAY. He was seventeen, like you. He was very dishy. We went to one of the barns. He was lovely about it.

RHONA. Was he a virgin?

LUKE. Yer don't go asking that.

RHONA. Why not? None of us are.

LUKE. Of course he was a virgin. It's why he was lovely.

RHONA. Well, I didn't know.

KAY. He wasn't a virgin when the afternoon was over, neither was I.

RHONA. I don't find virgins lovely. I don't know one.

AGNÈS *comes back. She has a bottle of champagne.*

KAY. Are you all right, Nan?

AGNÈS. Yes. I needed a breath of fresh air. You're very welcome, all of you.

AGNÈS *sits down. She gives the bottle to* RHONA.

For you, child. You can buy it here if you know where to go.

RHONA. You've embarrassed us now. Yer didn't have to.

AGNÈS. No, but I wanted to.

RHONA. I haven't paid for anything. None of us hardly has, except you.

AGNÈS. All this food is going cold.

They eat and drink.

NOEL. Can I have a look?

RHONA *gives him the bottle.*

Is it the same label as your time?

KAY. It's one of them, yes. Don't go on about it.

RHONA. Fucking hell, you could have owned that bottle.

KAY. No.

KAY *smiles.*

RHONA. Yer could. My baby could have as well, nearly. I'd be living in luxury with some minions. I'd do everything I liked and nothing else.

KAY. You do anyway.

RHONA. Wouldn't we be different people.

NOEL *puts the bottle on the floor.*

NOEL. You'd all be different people.

RHONA. That's what I said.

NOEL. Not quite.

RHONA *dunks some bread in the gravy.*

Would you have owned those bullocks, pet? Sorry, that was silly.

KAY. Why?

NOEL. How far does the land go. Does it go to the river?

KAY. It goes as far as Agnès' cottage and a little bit beyond.

NOEL. Not far then. It seems relatively small to support a château. It's amazing.

LUKE. The money comes from the history of the place, doesn't it.

KAY. Yes, it does.

RHONA. Who told yer that?

LUKE. Don't be dim, our kid.

RHONA. Was it the same when you lived here?

KAY. Almost exactly the same. It's barely changed.

RHONA. Don't you tell us to be dim. I'm not dim.

LUKE *looks at* AGNÈS.

LUKE. You're quiet.

AGNÈS. I am sometimes.

KAY. I should have brought some clean plates. We've gone and forgotten the cheese as well.

NOEL. I'm envious of you, Agnès. It's very peaceful. The river and the fields and the cows licking away on that purple cake they were putting out. I don't know what it does. The landscape. It's sort of simple, if I can put it like that without being superior. Then there's all the wine. I can see it might be lethal if I was about for long. We'll have to go and inspect the cellars, eh Rhona. You and me will have to make it our task to get some free samples to take home.

RHONA. You first before me.

KAY. Be careful where you go, Rhona. Remember it's private, won't you?

NOEL. I'll go first, pet. You follow and back me up. We're a team you and me.

Scene Four

A jetty on South Gare at the mouth of the river Tees. Two weeks later.

The wooden jetty comes out over the mudflats and water. It is rickety, with a plank or two missing, but safe to walk on. There is a heavy fog which is so dense that it is hard to penetrate it more than a few feet. The tide is coming in and the sea is lapping the shore.

NOEL *comes out of the white air. He walks towards the end of the jetty.*

RHONA *appears out of the fog. She is wearing her gaberdine. She takes off one of her muddy shoes.*

RHONA. You wear a pair of shoes once and they're ruined.

NOEL. You're as bad tempered as you were in France.

RHONA. I mean to be. Nobody's doing anything. I wouldn't mind if somebody was. We were shut out, us two. Something went on. Yer must have noticed. It's a secret kept from me.

NOEL. Me as well, Rhona.

RHONA *puts the shoe back on.*

RHONA. We've gone and lost her.

NOEL. She'll find us. We've been here before.

RHONA. Have yer? When?

NOEL. A couple of times. When the weather was better.

RHONA. It's supposed to be June, not winter.

NOEL. Be cheerful. It's not in your nature at the moment, is it.

RHONA. She's going back to France. Has she told you?

NOEL. I know, yes.

RHONA. I don't know why. We've only just got back a few days.

NOEL. A week.

RHONA. That's a few days, isn't it? She didn't ask me. It's all right for our Luke.

NOEL. She wants to go by herself this time.

RHONA. You know that Agnès. I thought she was useless.

NOEL. You're turning criticism into a hobby.

RHONA. I've every right.

NOEL. It belittles you. You belittle yourself.

RHONA. I had hopes, I did. It was pointless.

NOEL. Look after your dignity a bit more.

RHONA. Yes, dad.

NOEL *smiles.*

A foghorn sounds from the end of the gare three quarters of a mile away.

NOEL. Something did go on. I wasn't a party to it either. We've got to be tolerant.

RHONA. I'm no good at that. I'm best at the opposite.

NOEL. You think you're no good at most things. It's a self-fulfilling prophecy.

RHONA. Yer what?

NOEL. You know the spirit of what I'm saying. You're like your brother. Speak first, think later.

RHONA. Are you getting at us?

NOEL. Everyone gets at you much less than you imagine. The opposite.

RHONA. Yer mean yer like us?

NOEL. One day you'll give up all this.

RHONA. Only testing.

NOEL. Yes, you test people to their limits.

RHONA. I need loving, me. It's why I miss Jamie.

NOEL. Do you?

RHONA. Yeh.

NOEL. Let me give you some advice.

RHONA. Go on then. Tell me something I don't know.

NOEL. You've put me off now.

RHONA. I can't live the rest of me life not knowing.

NOEL. I was going to say, take affection when it's offered. It might not come along again.

RHONA. You're dead sweet, you are.

The fog is clearing. The bank on the landward side of the jetty is covered in couch grass.

KAY *enters along the gare. She is wearing a coat.*

KAY. I lost you both.

RHONA. What happened?

KAY. I realised I'd lost my watch.

KAY *pulls up her sleeve. Her watch is missing.*

I went back to look for it.

RHONA. Didn't yer get it?

KAY. No. It doesn't matter.

RHONA. Yes, it does.

The foghorn sounds.

KAY *comes onto the jetty.*

KAY. I thought you'd be here.

RHONA. Lovers' lane without the lane.

NOEL *puts his arm around her waist.*

KAY. I'm fine. There's nothing to fret about. Don't pet me, Noel.

NOEL. I'm sorry.

He takes his hand away.

KAY. It's only a watch. It has no sentimental value.

NOEL. I wasn't doing it for the watch.

KAY. On a clear day, Rhona, you can see right along the coast down to Redcar.

RHONA. What yer telling us for?

KAY. You were born less than ten miles away, and you don't know this area. It's such a pity.

RHONA. There's other places to go equally better.

NOEL. It's time for the big T, Rhona.

RHONA. What's that?

NOEL. Tolerance.

RHONA. Oh. Yeh.

The foghorn sounds.

I wouldn't be bothered if I hadn't ruined me shoes.

NOEL. Are you okay?

KAY. No, not really.

NOEL. What is it?

KAY. It's difficult.

KAY *takes her watch from her coat pocket.*

I didn't lose it.

RHONA. Had I better make myself scarce?

KAY. Would you mind?

RHONA. No.

RHONA *goes.*

NOEL. You shouldn't have done that in front of Rhona.

KAY. I didn't mean to. I was looking for an excuse to be on my own.

NOEL. You can be on your own whenever you want. You only have to say.

KAY. I know.

NOEL. What's the problem then?

A slight pause.

There must be a problem.

KAY. I don't want to have to say. I just want it to be.

NOEL. If you want to be by yourself more, it is fine. Stop worrying. I understand completely. I'm not an idiot. A lot went on in France, Kay. I didn't ask. I haven't pestered you at all. I've been very good, and I've felt small sometimes because of it. I reasoned, you know, that I'd leave it to you women. It wasn't that I didn't want to help if I could. Don't think that.

KAY. I don't. I know you would help. It's just you don't always help.

NOEL. Help who?

A slight pause.

I wish against a wish that we were talking about Jamie, but we're not. Why didn't you say?

KAY. I have.

NOEL *walks along the jetty.*

Wait a minute or two.

NOEL. I'm not a fool to be at the end of someone else's beck and call, Kay.

Silence.

In my own way, I quite love you. It's as honest as I can be.

KAY. Don't go soft on me.

NOEL. Why shouldn't I if I want to? You think about yourself often enough. I suppose my own way is peculiar, to some people at least. I don't mean it to be. Some people will always think some things of their choosing. It's up to them. I did my best.

KAY. I know.

NOEL. You hurt. You know how to hurt. You really do.

The foghorn sounds.

KAY. I have been trying to tell you for the last week or two, particularly in France. It was clear, wasn't it?

NOEL. Not to me. There was too much else going on. I put it down to Luke and his problems.

Silence.

Is this it, Kay?

KAY. I don't know. I don't know what to do.

A slight pause.

NOEL. Is it a bad day?

KAY. No. It was good as they go. It's turning bad.

A slight pause.

NOEL. I suppose I'm really asking you how much it's me.

KAY. I have to do what is right for Jamie.

NOEL. Of course you do. You are, pet. I'm involved somewhere, aren't I?

KAY. No.

NOEL *goes to her.*

NOEL. I don't mind if you want to go to France for a whole month. Be honest with me.

KAY. I am. You expect too much. I'm stuck.

A slight pause.

NOEL. It's Luke, isn't it? You think if you go back to Agnès you can both sort him out. He's the person who's stuck. You'll not change him. You wouldn't change him in a hundred years. Be realistic, Kay. As usual he's got everything he wants. He's expert at it. He's in France. You handed it to him on a plate. He doesn't care about you. He cares about himself. He always will. You're less than nothing in his eyes. See the truth for once, for goodness sake. You're no one's saviour.

The foghorn sounds.

KAY. I have to think about my son.

NOEL. You can forget about Luke then.

KAY. He's innocent.

NOEL. He had it coming to him, pet, one way or the other.

KAY. No.

NOEL. Yes.

KAY. No.

A motorboat is passing. The put-put of its outboard engine disturbs the quiet of the estuary.

NOEL. Why?

KAY. What?

NOEL. We could be so good together.

KAY. Good at what?

NOEL. Why, Kay? We've been terrific.

KAY. Have we?

NOEL. Not all the time. There isn't something wonderful to be had. You make the best of what there is.

KAY. No.

NOEL. Yes.

KAY. It's what you are. I won't be part of it. I have things I believe in. You don't.

KAY *walks along the jetty to the bank.*

Go home to your wife.

NOEL. Wait five minutes. Please.

KAY. Who for, Noel? For you or for me?

NOEL. Both of us. You are greedy. You really are.

KAY. There is no both of us. There never was. There never could be. I was going to use your wife, but I don't need to. It's over. It's easy.

KAY *walks up the bank and goes off along the gare.*

A pause.

NOEL *looks at the water.*

RHONA *comes on. She stops at the top of the jetty.* NOEL *turns.*

RHONA. I heard. I hate it when things alter. I like things to be the same, me.

RHONA *walks down the jetty.*

She gets at everyone. I wouldn't worry. She doesn't mean it. She gets at Jamie like that.

NOEL. Are you upset?

RHONA. Yeh, I am a bit. It must be because of the baby. I always want things to be smooth. I liked yer as a couple.

NOEL. She wasn't getting at you, Rhona.

RHONA. What?

NOEL. In France. Recently. All that niggling away. It turns out she was getting at me. Remember that.

RHONA. How d'yer mean?

NOEL. Think about it. It's all I ask.

RHONA. I will if I can. I don't suppose I can. I've forgotten already.

The foghorn sounds.

You know the worst thing? I don't know what to do. That's the worst thing. I've got no power.

NOEL *smiles.*

NOEL. You're a lovely lass. You're the best there is. You made France a real holiday.

RHONA. You don't fancy us, do yer?

NOEL. No.

RHONA. Honest? Yer'd say?

NOEL. Yes.

RHONA. I couldn't bear it if yer did, Noel. That's why I'm stupid with you sometimes. I think yer great, but all I care about is Jamie.

NOEL. I know, pet.

RHONA. He won't see the baby as it's born. That should be his right. I think it's the baby's right to see his father. I want him with me. I don't know how. I've thought and I've thought. I've thought and I've thought. That's it, all I've done is thought.

A slight pause.

NOEL. Are you better a bit?

RHONA. Yeh.

NOEL. Sure?

RHONA. Yeh.

NOEL. Positive?

RHONA. Yes.

Scene Five

The room in the château. A week later. An early morning in July.

Sunlight is streaming in through the windows in the sloping roof, lighting a single bed which is near the washbasin. LUKE *is in bed, covered by a white duvet that is reflecting some of the light, so that the room immediately surrounding him is very bright. He has his hands behind his head on the white pillows.*

JAMIE *is not far away, but at sufficient distance to be missing the full effect of the sun. He is wearing prison clothes, and his shoelaces are missing. He is holding up his trousers.*

LUKE. D'you ever imagine yourself to be where you're not, Jamie?

JAMIE *shrugs.*

JAMIE. I don't know. Yeh, I do sometimes. At night when I'm in bed.

LUKE. I've started to.

JAMIE *picks up a paperback book on the bed and flicks the pages.*

JAMIE. Are you still reading Stephen King books?

LUKE. Yeh. Keep it if you want.

JAMIE. No.

JAMIE *wanders about the room, looking at things.*

LUKE *gets up and sits on the side of the bed. His skin reflects the sunlight.*

LUKE. I was with your mam that afternoon. Kind of, anyway. Your mum as you call her. It was drizzling like it couldn't decide whether to rain or be fine. You can't know how we waited outside the court to find out where you were going, kid. The world could have been spinning out of control – maybe it was for you, but in a different way from us – and you would have had no idea what we were doing.

LUKE *picks up a pair of white pants off the floor and puts them on. He remains sitting.*

JAMIE *wanders to the bed.*

Are you okay?

JAMIE. Yeh.

LUKE. No lie?

JAMIE *sits on the edge of the bed next to* LUKE.

JAMIE. It's all right, once yer get used to it. Yer get yer dinner on time every day. They do your washing, and all the ironing. It's very handy having it all in one place.

LUKE. You'd say, Jamie?

JAMIE. Yeh.

LUKE. I've not been inside.

JAMIE. No.

LUKE. I have this dream, over and over, where I lose all me clothes on the first night. Even me dick isn't private. It's late because I've come from the court, and they've spent hours working out where to take me. It's the late at night bit of it that makes it scary.

JAMIE. Are you getting by?

LUKE. Yeh. Thanks for asking us though.

LUKE *picks up his jeans and puts them on. He remains sitting.*

Sometimes we sleep at the cottage, me and your nan. Sometimes I sleep here. It depends. Maybe in future I'll sleep here when I want to be with you. It can be like when we were boys, when yer mum let us stay and we'd sort of snuggle up close. I used to think I was getting close to your mum. It's daft, isn't it? It's how I knew I would love women, yer mum. I was always confused. I used to think it was me intelligence, that confusion. No one else did. Yer mum a lot. She saw something in me that I didn't see myself. It's too late now.

JAMIE *takes a tube of Smarties from his pocket.*

Any red ones?

JAMIE *gives him a red Smartie.* LUKE *eats it.* JAMIE *eats a handful.*

JAMIE. We used to sort out the colours with a torch under the eiderdown. D'you remember?

LUKE. Yeh, I do. I thought I was protecting you. I always did.

JAMIE. It's funny.

LUKE. What is?

JAMIE. I don't know. Yer seem in good spirits.

LUKE. Yeh.

JAMIE. You'd shout out if yer weren't, wouldn't you?

LUKE. Yeh.

JAMIE *gives* LUKE *a red Smartie.*

JAMIE. You don't have to go to the police, yer know. I don't want yer to. The reverse.

LUKE. Don't yer?

JAMIE. No. I've told everyone who'll listen. I'll never be a grass if I live to be a hundred.

JAMIE *eats some Smarties.* LUKE *stands up and goes to the washbasin. He turns on the taps and begins to clean his teeth.*

LUKE. You're great. You're the best.

JAMIE. Who is.

LUKE. You are. We'll always be mates.

JAMIE *gets up and walks to the open door.*

JAMIE. Luke.

LUKE. What?

JAMIE. You won't fret about me, will you? I couldn't take that. I can't stand being weedy. You've got to survive. You are.

LUKE. No. I promise. I'll see you when you come out. How about that, kid?

JAMIE. Yeh.

JAMIE *goes.*

LUKE *brushes his teeth.*

AGNÈS *enters. She is carrying the tray which is stacked with breakfast things, including a box of cornflakes and a jug of milk. She goes to the bed.*

AGNÈS. Luke. Luke.

LUKE *spits out some toothpaste.*

AGNÈS *puts the tray on the floor.*

KAY *enters. She has a holdall and her coat is across her arm.*

Catherine. My goodness you are early.

KAY. There was a bus in Paris and I caught it. Am I too soon?

AGNÈS. My dear, of course not.

KAY. I thought I saw you coming in here with breakfast. Hello, Luke. You're spoiling him rotten. I'm sure he doesn't deserve it.

KAY *puts down the bag and leaves the coat on top.*

AGNÈS. He is sound asleep.

KAY. He's what?

AGNÈS. He is asleep. This is what he does all the time. It is beginning to worry me.

LUKE *swishes out his mouth with water.*

KAY. Luke. Yoo-hoo.

KAY *joins* AGNÈS.

AGNÈS. There you are. Was he like this as a child?

KAY. If he was I can't remember, and I would remember.

LUKE *picks up some soap and washes with a flannel.*

AGNÈS. I am so pleased to see you, so happy you have come. Comment allez-vous?

KAY *shivers.*

KAY. Every time I come in here I shiver. Très bien, merci.

KAY *and* AGNÈS *kiss on both cheeks.*

AGNÈS. Have you eaten breakfast?

KAY. No. I'm not hungry.

AGNÈS. Would you like me to cook you some eggs?

AGNÈS *straightens the duvet on the bed.*

He will not eat them, so I have plenty in the cupboard.

AGNÈS *picks up the tray and takes it to the chest of drawers.*

I have some pork for lunch, or dinner, whichever you would like. I can get a chicken from the butcher if that is better.

KAY. I don't mind.

AGNÈS. I wish you would. It would be easier if you would say.

KAY. Do the pork. I can do it. I can help you. You're in a little bit of a tizz, Nan.

AGNÈS *goes to* LUKE. *She dries his face with a towel, and pushes him towards the bed.* LUKE *gets in.* AGNÈS *covers him with the duvet.*

The two women look at another.

AGNÈS. I am in a tizz.

AGNÈS *sits on the side of the bed.*

KAY. Am I being unfair?

AGNÈS. You are.

AGNÈS *gets up.*

That was my sit down.

KAY *smiles.*

KAY. You've done more than enough. I'm very grateful.

AGNÈS. Not enough. You do not understand, child. There is so much I should explain.

KAY. Explain what, Nan? You don't have to explain anything.

AGNÈS. I do. I should. I must. He will not go back, Catherine.

A slight pause.

KAY. Won't he? Are you sure?

AGNÈS. Yes.

KAY. Can't you make him? Persuade him?

AGNÈS. No. Can you?

KAY. I can try again.

AGNÈS. For what reason? I know for Jamie. It is up to him. I have tried with both of them.

KAY. Yes.

KAY *turns and walks away.*

AGNÈS. I know you blame me.

KAY. I don't. I really don't. Why should I blame you?

AGNÈS. I do not know why, but you do. This strangeness between us sometimes. It is still there wriggling away.

KAY. You're imagining it.

AGNÈS. No, I do not think so.

KAY. It doesn't matter.

AGNÈS. To me it does. You have expected so much.

KAY. Yes.

AGNÈS. I would like us to be friends.

KAY. We are. You're the only true friend I have. You're too honest, that's the problem.

A slight pause.

AGNÈS. I like him.

KAY. I know. I hate him. He does nothing but wrong.

AGNÈS. You are wrong.

KAY. You promised Jamie.

AGNÈS. I did not promise him anything.

KAY *walks to her bag.*

KAY. I knew he wouldn't come back, Nan. It didn't stop me hoping.

AGNÈS. It will be too late if you go. That will be it.

A slight pause.

KAY *picks up her coat and takes a tissue from the pocket. She blows her nose.*

KAY. I don't know how we got into this. I've only been here two minutes.

AGNÈS. I thought you were going.

KAY. No.

AGNÈS. Thank you.

KAY. Why?

AGNÈS. For staying.

KAY. Nan, I wouldn't walk away.

AGNÈS. You did a long time ago. You have done before.

A slight pause.

KAY. We're at cross purposes when we shouldn't be. It's so silly.

KAY *walks to* AGNÈS. AGNÈS *sits on the bed.*

AGNÈS. Oh, I wish I was strong. Stronger.

KAY. You are. We musn't fall out. It is not your problem any longer.

KAY *sits on the edge of the bed beside her.*

AGNÈS. I have made it my problem.

KAY. I asked you to. You have nothing to reproach yourself for.

AGNÈS. I must have. I have failed. I realise I have let Jamie down.

KAY. Jamie let himself down a long time ago. Or I did. It was always my problem, not yours. You are not responsible for any of this.

AGNÈS. I am. I must be. It feels as if I am. I go around in a daze, wondering how all this came about. So much has happened that I wish I understood even a little better. I would know what to do. Luke is very strong. He is manipulative. He is capable of good things, and very bad things. His instinct takes him into the bad things always, up to now. I do not know if I can make it better.

KAY. Stop. You'll wear yourself out. It's not fair.

AGNÈS *takes hold of* KAY*'s hands.*

AGNÈS. You are not listening to me. He means it when he says he loves me. He loves you in the same way. He does. It is very flattering.

KAY. I know. What are you trying to say, Nan?

AGNÈS. I have loved other people less. I have told him he can stay here.

KAY *frees her hands.*

KAY. I see.

AGNÈS. I thought you knew.

KAY. No.

AGNÈS. I wondered if you knew.

KAY. I didn't know anything.

KAY *stands up and walks away.*

I thought you were helping, not hindering.

AGNÈS *stands up.*

AGNÈS. I am not a saint.

KAY. Yes, I can see that.

AGNÈS. Why do you expect me to be? I admire his courage.

KAY. Is that all?

AGNÈS. He does have courage.

KAY. You're not the first person to be seduced by his charm, Nan, and I don't suppose you'll be the last.

AGNÈS. That is cruel.

KAY. Is it?

AGNÈS. Yes.

KAY. I don't care. If you can't see what he is, no one can help you.

AGNÈS. Why are you jealous?

KAY. Am I?

AGNÈS. Yes.

KAY. I'm not.

AGNÈS. A little.

KAY. No.

A slight pause.

AGNÈS. Why do you care about him more than Jamie?

KAY. I don't.

AGNÈS. I think you do. I think you always have.

KAY. You tell me, Nan.

AGNÈS. I am trying to be clear.

KAY. Are you?

LUKE *moves and changes position.*

AGNÈS. I think you understand very clearly.

LUKE *moves again.*

KAY. Have you slept with him?

AGNÈS. No.

KAY. That's something.

AGNÈS. We needed your say so.

KAY. What on earth are you talking about?

AGNÈS. He is a boy. I wanted your approval.

KAY. Boys will be boys. I don't suppose he's too bothered.

AGNÈS. Why are you being unkind?

KAY. I'm not. I'm being rational. One of us has to be.

LUKE *puts his hands behind his head on the pillows.*

LUKE. You've gone and woken us up now.

He puts his hands on the duvet and feels his legs. He pushes the duvet down and sees he is wearing jeans.

Have I been sleep walking again?

AGNÈS. Yes.

LUKE. What a fuck.

LUKE *pulls the duvet over his head and lies still on the bed.*

I know you're discussing me. Don't let me stop you. I don't want to spoil your fun.

A slight pause.

Can I ask you something, Kay.

KAY. What?

LUKE. It's only this. Why haven't you been to see Jamie?

KAY. Haven't I?

LUKE *pulls down the duvet.*

LUKE. No, you haven't.

KAY. No.

LUKE. If I was him I'd say all sorts of stuff. Most of it wouldn't be true. It'd be a test.

KAY. Would it, Luke?

LUKE. Yes.

KAY. You should know.

LUKE. You're right, I do know.

He gets out of bed. He rests his arm on AGNÈS*' shoulder.*

By the way, he wants to see you.

KAY *looks down.*

LUKE *puts his arm across* AGNÈS*' shoulder.*

We're in love, sort of, for the moment. One of us is. The other one of us pretends a bit because she cares about you. Something like that. It's all degrees, a bit of knowledge here, a bit of understanding there. It's all a mess. You're in a mess as much as us.

AGNÈS. Quiet, Luke.

LUKE. Why should I?

AGNÈS. Because you owe her something.

LUKE. Yes, I do.

AGNÈS *looks at him. She plays with his gold ear stud with her fingers.*

AGNÈS. You could be so good.

LUKE. I am trying to be all the time.

AGNÈS. Go to the police. Will you? Please. Please, Luke. I love you very much.

Silence.

LUKE. No.

AGNÈS. Yes.

LUKE. No.

AGNÈS. Yes.

LUKE. No.

A slight pause.

AGNÈS. Yes.

LUKE. I'll go if Jamie wants me to.

AGNÈS. Jamie does want you to, but he will never say.

LUKE. I know.

AGNÈS. Yes.

LUKE. I'll go if he says.

A slight pause.

KAY *goes to her coat and puts it on.*

AGNÈS. The bus turns round here and goes back to Paris.

KAY. I have a timetable.

AGNÈS *goes to her.*

AGNÈS. Will you stay for a day or two?

KAY. No, I can't.

AGNÈS. Will you write?

KAY. Yes.

KAY *picks up her holdall and goes out.*

LUKE. Did yer get her permission? I'm dying for it. I reckon it's why I'm sleep walking.

AGNÈS *looks at him.*

AGNÈS. Yes, I think I did.

Scene Six

The visitor's room at Deerbolt. A few days later.

Sunlight is streaming in through the window onto the trestle-table.

KAY *is there, standing waiting. She is wearing a sleeveless cotton dress.*

The door opens and JAMIE *comes in. There is a belt on his trousers and laces in his shoes. He closes the door. He looks down.*

KAY. Hello.

JAMIE. Hello.

A slight pause.

What d'you want, Mum?

KAY. To see you.

JAMIE *looks up.*

JAMIE. You've seen. Why?

KAY *goes to him.* JAMIE *moves away.*

Don't touch me.

JAMIE *goes to the table and sits down. He lights a cigarette.*

A pause.

KAY *goes to the table and sits down opposite him.*

A slight pause.

JAMIE *clenches his fist, leans forward and thumps hard into the top of her arm. He walks away, leaving the cigarette burning in the ashtray.*

A pause.

KAY *gets up and goes to him.* JAMIE *thumps her again. He goes to the table but does not sit down. He picks up the cigarette and smokes. His hand is red and shaking slightly.*

A slight pause.

KAY. I'm sorry.

JAMIE. What are you sorry for?

A slight pause.

You don't know what it's like in here. There's criminals everywhere yer go. Yer can't escape them. Yer can't escape. If anyone can escape it should be me. They should let me out. I'm more innocent than Jesus.

KAY. I know.

JAMIE. You haven't done nowt. No one has. I should be on television, but I'm not. That jury was against us from the second they walked in. There was only one of them who listened, and he didn't do owt, far as I know. The judge didn't give them permission to say I wasn't guilty. He should have done, at least a bit. It's not fair.

A slight pause.

KAY. Yes, it isn't fair.

JAMIE. You didn't support us. Not really. I had to support myself or no one would have done. I'm supporting myself now, doing a bit of education. It's been a shock, I can tell yer. I'm only doing education because you get to be on your own. I'd do car mechanics, except there're loads of them, and only one car.

A slight pause.

KAY. What are you doing?

JAMIE. How d'you mean?

KAY. In education.

JAMIE. Geography.

KAY. Is that all?

JAMIE. Yeh.

KAY. You passed that anyway.

JAMIE. That's why I'm doing it, for the record, for parole.

KAY. You could do English and history and maths, and chemistry.

JAMIE. No. I can't be bothered. They only do geography at the moment.

KAY. Are you sure?

JAMIE. Don't know. It is 'A' level, Mum. I won't pass or anything.

A slight pause.

KAY. I didn't realise you were talking about 'A' level.

JAMIE. What's the point of doing the other again?

KAY. Yes.

JAMIE. I've got the certificate already, somewhere.

KAY. It's in the top drawer in the sideboard.

JAMIE. I wondered where it had gone.

KAY. It's beneath the cutlery.

JAMIE. Will yer keep it for us?

KAY. I'm not going to throw it away.

JAMIE. Thanks.

A slight pause.

KAY. Why won't you pass?

JAMIE. I'm no good at it.

KAY. You will if you try hard. You're capable enough.

JAMIE. No.

A slight pause.

You'd better go, Mum. You don't want to be seen with me.

A slight pause.

KAY. Seen by who? There is only us.

JAMIE. You know what I mean, don't you?

A slight pause.

KAY. Yes, I do know what you mean.

JAMIE. It doesn't matter any more. There's no point.

KAY. It does to me.

KAY *goes towards him.*

JAMIE. Go away. Go home, Mum. I don't want you. You'll only get upset if you know. There's prisoners in here who don't give a toss. You don't turn your back. You show a little bit of feeling for someone else. You're dead.

KAY. No.

JAMIE. Yes.

KAY. I don't think so.

JAMIE. I know, I'm telling yer. It's what it is.

KAY. There is a beginning, Jamie.

JAMIE. I'm innocent, Mum. It's not fair.

KAY. No one else has to know.

JAMIE. Know what?

KAY. No one else is in here.

A slight pause.

JAMIE. You could tell us I'm doing okay. That would help.

KAY. You're doing more than okay.

JAMIE. Am I?

KAY. Yes.

JAMIE. It's the first time you've said that. I've not grassed, you know.

KAY. I know.

JAMIE. I've wanted to an' all.

KAY. Have you?

JAMIE. Yes.

KAY. I know. You musn't.

JAMIE. I won't. I know I won't. I'm doing okay. I'm getting by. I'll never grass.

KAY. You were never a grass, Jamie.

JAMIE. Wasn't I? I felt like I was.

KAY. No.

JAMIE. I don't know why. I haven't grassed, have I?

KAY. Of course not.

JAMIE. It's a bit of relief, Mum.

A pause.

KAY. Come here. Please.

JAMIE *goes to her.*

JAMIE. What d'you want?

KAY. I don't know what I want.

KAY *takes hold of his hand. She moves her fingers up his arm.*

What I want I can't have.

JAMIE. What's that?

KAY. You to be at home.

The end.